PRINCIPLES OF INSURANCE

AS PER CBCS SYLLABUS

DR. ZAKER UL OMAN | MOHD. MANSOOR HUSSAIN | SOMNATH CHATTOPADHYAY

Contents

Principles Of Insurance

As per new CBCS Restructured Syllabus for B.Com, (Sec-2 Common for All Streams) 2nd Year 3rd Semester for All the Universities in Telangana State.

(w.e.f. 2019-20)

Dr. Zaker Ul Oman,

M.Com., MBA., PhD

Assistant Professor of Commerce and Business Management,

Avinash College of Commerce,

Himayathnagar, Hyderabad

Mr. Mansoor Hussain,

M.Com., MBA., CA-IPCC

Assistant Professor of Commerce and Business Management,

Avinash College of Commerce,

Himayathnagar, Hyderabad

Mr. Somnath Chattopadhyay,

MA-Eco., M.Com., MBA., CA-Inter

Associate Professor of Commerce and Business Management,

Avinash College of Commerce,

Himayathnagar, Hyderabad

Foreword

The world we live in is full of uncertainties. From unforeseen events that threaten our financial well-being to the natural course of life itself, the potential for loss is ever-present. Insurance emerges as a powerful tool in navigating these uncertainties, providing a safety net and offering peace of mind. This book serves as your comprehensive guide to the world of insurance. It delves deep into the core concepts of risk management, taking you on a journey from understanding the different types of risks to exploring how insurance helps minimize their impact.

The book lays a solid foundation by explaining the basic building blocks of insurance. You'll gain a clear understanding of pooling of risks, the various classes of insurance available, and the importance of this crucial financial instrument for both individuals and society as a whole.

Demystifying the insurance market is a key focus. The book unveils its participants, from insurance companies and intermediaries to regulatory bodies. By understanding their roles and responsibilities, you'll be empowered to navigate the insurance landscape with confidence.

The intricacies of insurance products are explored, equipping you with the knowledge to make informed decisions. You'll learn about the distinct characteristics of life insurance and general insurance products, enabling you to choose the ones that best suit your needs. The book also delves into the legal aspects of insurance contracts, explaining crucial principles like insurable interest, indemnity, and utmost good faith.

This book goes beyond merely providing information. It emphasizes the importance of ethical behavior in the insurance industry, highlighting the role of customer needs and satisfaction. Understanding these aspects fosters a healthy insurance ecosystem that benefits both policyholders and insurers.

Embrace the journey from risk to security. Let this book be your guide.

Dr. YSS Savitri Devi

Preface

The world around us is full of uncertainties. From the risk of losing a loved one to the fear of property damage, these uncertainties can cause significant financial and emotional stress. Insurance emerges as a powerful tool to navigate these risks, offering protection and peace of mind.

This book is designed to be your comprehensive guide to the world of insurance. Whether you're a student seeking a solid foundation in insurance fundamentals, a professional looking to enhance your understanding, or simply an individual wanting to make informed decisions about your financial security, this book caters to your needs.

This book takes you on a journey through the core concepts of insurance. We begin by exploring the very nature of risk and delve into various techniques to minimize its impact. We then introduce insurance as a risk management tool, explaining its evolution and core principles.

The book delves into the intricate workings of the insurance market, introducing you to its various participants – insurance companies, intermediaries, and regulators – and their roles. We equip you with essential insurance terminology, enabling you to navigate communication with insurance providers effectively.

Understanding your needs as an insurance customer is paramount. We explore various life and general insurance products available, catering to diverse risks like death, property damage, financial losses due to accidents or hospitalization.

Finally, we delve into the legal framework of insurance contracts, explaining key principles such as insurable interest, indemnity, and utmost good faith. These principles ensure fairness and transparency in the relationship between you and the insurance company.

Learning Approach:

This book emphasizes a clear and concise approach. We break down complex concepts into easily understandable terms, using practical examples to illustrate key points.

Learning Outcome:

By the end of this course, you will be able to explain core insurance concepts like risk, pooling, and insurable interest. You'll differentiate life and general insurance products, understanding how they address risks of death, longevity, property damage, and financial losses. You'll grasp key principles governing insurance contracts, ensuring fair dealings between policyholders and insurers. This foundation will equip you to analyze the role of insurance in risk management, economic development, and social security.

Beyond the Book:

While this book provides a strong foundation, the ever-evolving insurance landscape demands continuous learning. We encourage you to utilize the resources provided at the end of each chapter for further exploration.

Embrace this journey of understanding insurance. With the knowledge gained, you'll be empowered to make informed decisions and navigate the world of financial security with confidence.

Dr. Zaker Ul Oman
Mohd. Mansoor Ahmed
Somnath Chattopadhyay

Acknowledgements

The completion of this book, "Principles of Insurance," would not have been possible without the invaluable support and inspiration of several individuals. We are deeply grateful to **Dr. Avinash Brahmadevara, Chairman** of Avinash Group of Institutionswhose leadership and unwavering commitment to academic excellence fostered the environment that allowed this project to flourish. **Dean Academics AGI Dr. Susheela Kanduri** for her constant encouragement and belief in our ability to contribute to the field of academic education. **Principal Dr. YSS Savitri Devi, ACC Himayatnagar** for providing the necessary resources and creating a positive learning atmosphere that spurred the development of this book. **Ms. BS Deepa, HoD, ACC Himayatnagar** whose guidance and expertise in academics proved invaluable throughout the writing process.

We are particularly indebted to **Notion Press** for recognizing the potential of this book and offering us the opportunity to publish it with such a prestigious organization.

We are also thankful to our colleagues and reviewers who provided valuable feedback and suggestions that significantly improved the quality of the manuscript.

Finally, we extend our heartfelt gratitude to our families and loved ones for their unwavering support and understanding throughout this journey.

We hope this book serves as a valuable resource for students and professionals alike, and we dedicate it to all those who have contributed to its creation.

Dr. Zaker Ul Oman
Mohd. Mansoor Hussain
Somnath Chattopadhyay

CHAPTER ONE

RISK MANAGEMENT AND INSURANCE

1.1 Risk Management

1.1.1 Basic Concept of Risk

Financial Risk stands as a significant worry for businesses across various sectors and regions. This concern has led to the widespread recognition of the Financial Risk Manager FRM Exam among financial professionals worldwide. The FRM credential is considered the premier achievement for those in risk management globally. Understanding Financial Risk is fundamental to the FRM Level 1 exam. Before delving into methods for managing risk and executing risk management strategies, it's crucial to grasp the concept of risk and its various types.

Risk is described as an event that negatively affects profitability and/or reputation due to multiple sources of uncertainty. It's essential that the managerial process identifies and accounts for both the uncertainty and potential negative impacts on profitability and/or reputation.

Risk is an integral part of every business's vocabulary, and its comprehension and management are of utmost importance. This is particularly true in the banking sector, where risk is inherent in the operations. Given the critical nature of risk management, it's no surprise that it is currently under intense scrutiny from global banking regulators.

Regulatory bodies such as the Bank of International Settlements (BIS), the Federal Reserve in the United States, Bundesbank in Germany, and Reserve Bank of India have voiced their concerns regarding the risk-taking behaviours of banks. These concerns are heightened by the increasingly risky environment, marked by volatile exchange rates and interest rates, as well as the international spread of bank capital in search of returns.

The banking sector's exposure to corporations in Asia and Latin America has significantly increased compared to previous years. This has led regulators to worry about the banks' resilience to withstand these challenges. Furthermore, the collapse of well-known banks like Barings and the losses suffered due to flawed option pricing models at NatWest Markets have only added to the regulatory focus on capital and reporting requirements.

Banks, both for-profit and not-for-profit, place their tangible and intangible assets at risk to achieve their goals. Whether the organization is profit-driven or not, the responsibility of management is to navigate these risks in an uncertain environment. As a result, the role of organizational management has become synonymous with risk management.

1.1.2 Understanding Risk

The Oxford Dictionary of Word Origin explains the origin of the term "risk" as follows: "The direct source of the word risk is well-known. The English adopted the term "risqué" from French in the 17th century, which itself was derived from Italian rischo, originating from the Latin verb rischare, meaning 'to run into danger'.

However, beyond this, we enter into uncertain territory. One theory suggests that it originated from a nautical context, referring to ships that faced the danger of getting too close to hazardous rocky shores. This theory is supported by evidence such as the Greek word rhiza, meaning a cliff, and the Latin verb resecure, which means 'to cut of short' (referring to a rocky cliff as land that has been 'cut off short'), both of which have been proposed as the roots of rischare.

Taking risks is a natural inclination for banks. Banks participate in the process of financial intermediation by assuming risks to earn more than their return to depositors. Risk is an event or harm that could damage an institution's earnings and/or reputation. It is akin to energy, which cannot be created or destroyed but can only be transferred or controlled.

There's a direct link between risk and reward, and the pursuit of maximizing profits has led to an increase in risk-taking for greater rewards. Regardless of the type of risk, its impact is primarily financial. In the end, risk is inevitable. The extent and nature of risk associated with each transaction are not always predictable.

All banks, along with their individual bankers, must recognize that risk is an unavoidable aspect of business. The nature and magnitude of risk linked to each transaction cannot be precisely determined. The risk management models that exist are primarily based on past occurrences, which may or may not be repeated in the future. Risk is inherent to the business world. Since it cannot be eliminated, it must be managed.

1.1.3 Understanding Risk Characteristics

Banking involves the process of intermediating funds, which inherently carries risks. To generate profits and achieve a margin, bankers often engage in positions within the investment market or the loan sector. It's clear that risk is a necessary component for the possibility of profit. As previously mentioned, there's a direct link between risk and potential gain. The primary reason for businesses to embrace risk is the pursuit of profit. Risks come in various forms but share certain common traits.

Financial Risk is distinct from actual loss. Typically, the risks associated with business activities are well-known. These risks are probabilistic and universal. Financial risks in markets are events that are likely to occur. The uncertainty lies more in the timing and the magnitude of these events.

There's no guarantee of complete success or failure. There's always an element of uncertainty, which is reflected in probability. Risk is universal. For instance, one could say, "the likelihood of a chemical unit in a specific industrial area succeeding is low." No one can definitively predict whether a particular chemical unit will succeed or fail.

Risks are identifiable, although not always quantifiable. Risk and return are directly related; in other words, higher risk often leads to higher return, and vice versa. This is why risk is essential for business operations. The risks discussed below are interconnected; they cover all possible outcomes but do not exclude each other.

1.1.4 Evolving Forms of Risk

Risk is inherent in every business endeavour. It's particularly noticeable and significant in the financial sector, especially banks. In a controlled financial system, risk may not be as apparent. Risk management in such conditions might lack organization. However, with globalization, there's been a shift from ad hoc to systematic and structured policy approaches. New strategies like 'anticipate/prevent/monitor mitigate' have replaced the traditional approach of 'inspect/detect/react.' The focus is now more on procedures rather than individuals. This shift has introduced numerous challenges for banks. Given this context, it's important to explore the various types of risks faced by banks.

1.2 Types of Risks

Risk can be described as the probability of experiencing an unexpected or adverse outcome. Any action or activity that could result in a loss is considered a risk. Risks can be classified into three broad categories: Business Risk, Non-Business Risk, and Financial Risk.

a. **Business Risk:** These risks are assumed by companies to increase the value for shareholders and profits. For instance, businesses take on high-cost risks in marketing to introduce a new product, aiming for greater sales.
b. **Non-Business Risk:** These risks are beyond the control of companies. They stem from political and economic imbalances, which are considered non-business risks.
c. **Financial Risk:** Financial risk refers to the potential for financial loss for companies. It typically stems from instability and losses in the financial markets, driven by fluctuations in stock prices, exchange rates, and interest rates, among others.

1.2.1 Types of Financial Risks

Financial risk is a critical category of risk for all businesses. It is triggered by market movements, which can be influenced by various factors. Consequently, financial risk can be categorized into several types, including Market Risk, Credit Risk, Liquidity Risk, Operational Risk, and Legal Risk.

a. **Market Risk:** This risk is associated with changes in the prices of financial assets. It can be further divided into Directional Risk and Non-Directional Risk. Directional risk is caused by movements in stock prices, interest rates, and more. Non-Directional risk, on the other hand, is related to volatility.
b. **Credit Risk:** This risk occurs when a party fails to meet their obligations to another party. Credit risk can be further divided into Sovereign Risk and Settlement Risk. Sovereign risk typically results from challenging foreign exchange policies, while settlement risk emerges when one party makes a payment but the other fails to fulfill their obligations.
c. **Liquidity Risk:** This risk arises from the inability to carry out transactions. It can be further categorized into Asset Liquidity Risk and Funding Liquidity Risk. Asset Liquidity Risk is due to a lack of sufficient buyers or sellers for sell orders and buy orders, respectively. Funding Liquidity Risk, on the other hand, is caused by a shortage of available funds.
d. **Operational Risk:** This risk is linked to operational failures, such as mismanagement or technical issues. Operational risk can be further divided into Fraud Risk and Model Risk. Fraud risk is the result of inadequate controls, while Model Risk is due to the incorrect application of models.
e. **Legal Risk:** This type of financial risk is the result of legal constraints, such as lawsuits. When a company incurs financial losses due to legal actions, it is facing legal risk.

1.3 Actual and consequential losses

1.3.1 Actual Loss

The term "actual loss" in insurance refers to the real costs or expenses resulting from a claim. According to the terms of the insurance policy, it represents the insurance company's whole payment for the whole loss or claim. When property that is insured is destroyed or damaged to the point that it cannot be repaired or recovered for use, it is said to have suffered an actual total loss. Usually, a real total loss sets off the highest payout allowed by the conditions of the insurance policy. Actual loss refers to how much money has been paid out by the insurance company on behalf of the damage caused to your property by the insured perils in a claim.

To identify the percentage of the expenditure that is directly related to a claim, the phrase "actual loss" is sometimes used. Rather than the full cost or value claimed during the loss, that sum will be reimbursed.

Often, the real loss is unknown until the claim has been thoroughly evaluated and is about to close.

It includes

Costs for contractors or other specialists

- Additional living expenses

- Costs of repairs
- Debris removal
- Storage of items (if applicable)

Sec. 57(1) of the Marine Insurance Act 1906, which states that there is an actual total loss where the subject matter insured is destroyed or so damaged as to cease to be a thing of the kind insured, or where the assured is irretrievably deprived thereof, applies to any subject matter insured within a marine insurance policy. This may include, among other things, ship, goods, freight, profits and commissions, wages, and disbursements.

1.3.2 Consequential Losses

A consequential loss is an unintended negative effect brought on by harm to equipment or commercial property. A company owner can receive coverage for secondary losses in addition to purchasing insurance to cover any damage to equipment and property. The owner will get compensation for this lost company income under a consequential loss insurance or clause.
Business income or business interruption insurance are other names for this kind of coverage.

Consequential loss is the term used to describe any disruption in business operations brought on by fire or other unique risks that results in various types of financial loss. The owner is financially compensated for the lost revenue from the business in the event of a fire by means of a consequential loss insurance policy for fire or other unique dangers.

Fire incidents have the ability to affect ongoing and ongoing projects in addition to harming inventory and equipment. Financial loss and company disruption may result from this. A standard fire and special hazards policy, for example, covers fire and related dangers but excludes financial damage from business disruption. Herein lies the role of consequential loss insurance.

1.3.3 Functions

a. Should a loss occur due to fire or other specific risks, leading to a reduction in earnings or income, or an increase in fixed expenses that are covered by the policy, the insured individual must promptly contact the insurance company's toll-free line to file a claim.
b. Following this, the insurance company will review the Final Survey Report (FSR) provided by the assigned Surveyor and determine the compensation amount for the organization, adhering to the policy's conditions.
c. The insurance company will take into account the organization's annual gross profit, the chosen indemnity period, and any additional coverage options when setting the premium for consequential loss insurance.
d. A licensed surveyor will be hired to assess the situation and review the relevant documents to accurately evaluate the loss suffered by the organization.

The insurance policy offers protection against various types of business losses:

i. Payments for layoffs and retrenchment
ii. Loss of total profit due to a drop in sales
iii. Costs for auditors
iv. Losses from spoiled goods

1.4 Risk Management

1.4.1 Risk Management Process

The risk management process serves as a guide for the steps required to manage risks effectively. It consists of five fundamental stages: risk identification, risk analysis, risk prioritization, risk mitigation, and risk monitoring. These stages are collectively known as the risk management process. Initially, risks are identified within the business's operational environment, encompassing various categories such as legal, environmental, market, regulatory, and more. It's crucial to pinpoint as many risk factors as possible. In traditional systems, each stage demands extensive documentation and administrative work.

However, in a digital setting, the process becomes more streamlined.

Step-1: Identify the Risk

For instance, in the first step, risk identification, all relevant information is directly entered into the system. This approach ensures that all stakeholders have access to the risk information, eliminating the need to request reports through email. This accessibility allows anyone interested in viewing identified risks to do so directly from the risk management system.

Step-2: Analyze the Risk

In the second step, risk analysis, the extent of the risk's impact is assessed. This involves understanding the risk's relationship with various organizational factors and determining its severity and impact on business operations. While some risks could potentially halt business operations, others might only cause minor disruptions. In a manual risk management system, this analysis is performed manually.

When a risk management strategy is put into action, one of the crucial initial steps involves linking risks to various documents, policies, procedures, and business operations. This implies that the system will be equipped with a framework that maps risks, allowing for the assessment of risks and the understanding of their wide-ranging impacts.

Step 3: Assess or Order the Risk Level

It's crucial to assess and prioritize risks. Risk management strategies often categorize risks based on their potential impact, ranging from minor inconveniences to major losses. Risks that could cause minor disruptions are typically given a lower priority, while those with the potential for catastrophic damage are considered the highest priority. Ranking risks is essential for understanding the overall exposure of the organization to various risks. While the organization might face multiple minor risks, it might not need top-level management's immediate attention. Conversely, a single high-priority risk could necessitate urgent action.

Step 4: Address the Risk

Every risk must be either mitigated or contained to the greatest extent possible. This involves collaborating with experts in the relevant field. In a manual setting, this process includes reaching out to all stakeholders and organizing meetings to discuss the issues. However, this often leads to a fragmented approach, with discussions spread across numerous email threads, documents, spreadsheets, and phone calls. In a risk management system, all stakeholders can receive notifications directly from the system. Discussions about the risk and potential solutions can occur within the system, allowing upper management to oversee the proposed solutions and their progress. This eliminates the need for stakeholders to individually contact each other for updates, providing a more streamlined approach.

Step 5: Track and Review the Risk

Not all risks can be completely eliminated; some are inherent and must be continuously monitored. Examples include market risks and environmental risks. In manual systems, risk monitoring is typically handled by dedicated employees who must vigilantly watch for changes in risk factors. In a digital setting, the risk management system oversees the entire risk framework of the organization, making any changes immediately visible to all. Computers are more effective at continuous risk monitoring than humans. This approach to risk monitoring ensures the business's continuity.

1.5 Types of Insurance

1.5.1 Categorization of General Insurance Firms

General insurance, also known as non-life insurance, encompasses policies like car and home insurance that pay out based on the financial impact of a specific event. It is generally understood as any insurance not classified as life insurance. In the United States and Canada, it's referred to as property and casualty insurance, while in Continental Europe, it's known as non-life insurance.

Various Forms of General Insurance in India:

a. Health Insurance

Digit Health Insurance provides coverage for medical expenses related to hospital stays due to accidents or illnesses. Each policy is unique, but it typically includes:

1. Insurance for hospital stays following accidents
2. Insurance for illnesses and hospital stays
3. Insurance for daycare procedures
4. Insurance for psychiatric care
5. Insurance for annual health check-ups
6. Insurance for daily cash benefits at the hospital

b. Travel Insurance

Travel Insurance protects you financially against any liabilities that may arise while traveling within or outside India. These liabilities could be medical or non-medical in nature. The policy can cover travel for up to 180 days in a year, with the option to take multiple trips within the same year. It includes:

1. Protection against lost luggage
2. Protection against lost passports
3. Protection against hijacking
4. Protection against medical emergencies
5. Protection against flight delays
6. Protection against accidental deaths
7. Protection for activities like adventure sports

c. Motor Insurance

Motor Insurance is split into two categories: two-wheeler and four-wheeler vehicle insurance.

To legally drive in India, it's mandatory to have a Motor Insurance Policy. There are two main types: a) Third-Party Liability and b) Comprehensive Package Policy.

A Third-Party Policy covers damages or liabilities to others if your vehicle causes damage to their property, person, or another vehicle. This is the bare minimum requirement to drive legally in India, as per the Motor Vehicles Act.

A Comprehensive Package Policy, on the other hand, covers damages or liabilities to others as well as damages or losses to your own vehicle. This includes accidents, theft, fire, natural disasters, and more.

Digit Insurance offers several add-ons for its Comprehensive Package Policies for cars and motorcycles, providing extra protection for your vehicle, such as:

i. Insurance for tire protection
ii. Insurance for zero depreciation
iii. Insurance for return to invoice
iv. Insurance for engine and gearbox protection
v. Insurance for breakdown assistance

d. Marine Insurance

During transit by rail, road, sea, or air, marine cargo insurance guards against loss or damage to commodities, freight, and other interests.

e. Home Insurance

Every purchase you make is a treasure that you cherish, and therefore, it deserves protection. A Home Insurance Policy safeguards your valuable possessions and other assets with a complete coverage plan.

Digit Insurance offers protection for your home against theft, loss, damage to jewellery, fire, and natural disasters.

f. Commercial Insurance

The insurance categories that impact business operations in tangible ways are known as Commercial Insurance. The types of insurance coverage available include:

1. Property Insurance
2. Engineering Insurance
3. Liability Insurance
4. Marine Insurance
5. Employee Benefit Insurance
6. Business Interruption Insurance

1.5.2 Comparing Life Insurance with Other Insurance Types

Life Insurance is a contract between the insurance company or government that promises compensation for the loss of life in exchange for a premium payment. The beneficiary named in the policy receives the specified amount from the insurer if the insured person passes away.

1.5.3 Different Types of Life Insurance Policies

1. **Term Insurance Plan:** These plans are purchased for a specific duration, such as 20 or 30 years. Since they lack cash value and no maturity benefits, they are more affordable than other policies. They only become beneficial if the event occurs, i.e., the insured person's death.
2. **Endowment Policy:** Similar to Term Insurance Plans, Endowment Policies also have a maturity benefit. However, they also provide a lump sum payout if the insured person survives until the policy's maturity date. The details of both policies are the same.
3. **Unit Linked Insurance Plan:** These plans allow the policyholder to accumulate wealth in addition to life insurance coverage. The premium paid is divided into two parts: one for life insurance and another for wealth accumulation. The plan also offers the option to partially withdraw the amount.
4. **Money Back Policy:** This policy is like an Endowment Policy, with the additional benefit of survival benefits that are distributed over the policy term.
5. **Whole Life Policy:** Unlike other policies that have an expiration date, Whole Life Policies last the insured person's entire life. They also provide survival benefits. The policyholder has the option to partially withdraw the sum insured and borrow against the policy.
6. **Annuity/ Pension Plan:** In this plan, the premium collected is invested as assets, and the policyholder receives income in the form of annuity or a lump sum, depending on their choice.

1.5.4 Advantages of Life Insurance

1. **Protection Against Risks:** Life insurance offers protection against risks to the insured's family by providing them with financial compensation in exchange for the premiums paid.
2. **Various Plans for Various Purposes:** Life insurance providers offer a variety of plans tailored to the insured's specific needs, with more comprehensive plans typically requiring higher premiums.
3. **Coverage for Medical Expenses:** These policies also include coverage for medical bills and treatments for critical illnesses.
4. **Encourages Savings and Wealth Accumulation:** Life insurance policies may also include savings plans, where your money is invested in profitable ventures.
5. **Secured Income:** Life insurance policies guarantee a specific sum assured amount that will be paid out upon the occurrence of the event.
6. **Loan Provision:** Life insurance companies allow the insured to borrow a specific amount, a feature available only on certain policies.
7. **Tax Advantages:** The premiums paid for life insurance are tax-deductible under section 80C of the Income Tax Act, 1961.

1.5.5 Key Concepts of Life Insurance

Life insurance operates on several fundamental concepts designed to balance the needs of the insurance provider for profitability with the insured's desire for protection and financial security. These concepts include:

1. **Insurable Interest:** This concept relates to the degree of interest an individual has in a specific insurance policy. It can be based on familial ties, personal relationships, and more. The level of interest determines whether an insurance company will approve or deny an application to prevent policy misuse.
2. **Law of Large Numbers:** This principle ensures stability and reduces long-term losses by applying statistical theories to large-scale data sets.
3. **Good Faith:** The act of purchasing insurance is seen as a contractual agreement between the insurer and the insured. It's essential that both parties are honest and transparent. Misrepresenting information to the insurer can lead to severe consequences for the insured in the future. Therefore, the insurer must clearly explain all policy details, ensuring there are no hidden or unexpected terms, and the insured is fully informed about all conditions.
4. **Risk & Minimal Loss:** Insurance is inherently risky, and insurance companies must operate to make profits while managing these risks. The principle of minimal risk encourages the insured to take steps to minimize their exposure to potential hazards. This includes taking necessary precautions to avoid risks.

1.5.6 Process for Claim Settlement

Should the event occur, the person receiving the benefit must promptly submit the claim notification form to the insurance company. This form should include details such as the date, location, and cause of death. Upon receiving the claim notification form, the insurance company may request further information on:

1. Certificate of Death
2. Copies of the Insurance Policy
3. Legal Proof of Ownership if the insured individual did not appoint a beneficiary
4. Assignment Deeds

After all the necessary documents are submitted, the insurance company will verify the claim and proceed with its settlement.

1.5.7 Key Considerations for Life Insurance

1. **Research:** As a potential life insurance applicant, there are a variety of policy options available. It's crucial to conduct thorough research before deciding on a policy, as this can help you save money and ensure you receive the best benefits.
2. **Review Terms and Conditions:** The terms and conditions of a life insurance policy outline all the important details about the policy. It's important to read these terms carefully and fully understand them before committing to a policy.
3. **Be Aware of Lock-In Periods:** Sometimes, individuals purchase life insurance policies without fully understanding them and later regret their decision. In such cases, some insurance companies offer a lock-in period, which is typically a short timeframe (1-5 days) during which the policyholder can return the policy and choose another if they are not satisfied with the initial purchase.
4. **Consider Payment Options for Premiums:** Most insurance companies provide various options for premium payments, including annual, semi-annual, quarterly, or monthly. It's advisable to choose an Electronic Check System (ECS) payment method, which will automatically deduct the required insurance amount from your bank account on a regular basis. Additionally, you can select a payment schedule that suits your convenience.
5. **Be Complete in Your Application:** It's important to be honest and accurate when filling out the life insurance application form. All personal information and medical history should be provided truthfully. Misrepresenting information can lead to complications when attempting to file a claim later on.

1.5.8 Leading Life Insurance Providers in India

Here are some of the leading life insurance providers in India:

1. LIC — Life Insurance Corporation
2. SBI Life Insurance
3. ICICI Prudential Life Insurance
4. HDFC Standard Life Insurance
5. Bajaj Allianz Life Insurance
6. Max Life Insurance
7. Birla Sun Life Insurance
8. Kotak Life Insurance

We all face uncertainties about the future, and while we hope for the best, it's important to be ready for unexpected events. A life insurance policy serves as a financial safety net, ensuring your loved ones are financially secure. Therefore, a life insurance policy is a relatively small investment in exchange for the significant peace of mind it provides.

1.6 The Significance of Insurance

1.6.1 Life Insurance

The insurance industry in India has undergone significant transformations, moving from a competitive, open market to nationalization and then back to a more liberalized state. A detailed examination of the evolution of the Indian insurance sector over nearly two centuries highlights the comprehensive changes it has experienced.

A Historical Overview of the Insurance Sector

The concept of life insurance in India as we know it today originated in 1818 with the founding of the Oriental Life Insurance Company in Calcutta.

Key milestones in the life insurance sector in India include:

1. **1912:** The enactment of the Indian Life Assurance Companies Act, marking the first legislation to regulate the life insurance sector.
2. **1928:** the passing of the Indian Insurance firms Act, which made it easier for the government to compile statistics on firms that offer both life and non-life insurance.
3. **1938:** The consolidation and amendment of existing laws under the Insurance Act, with the goal of safeguarding the interests of policyholders.
4. **1956:** The central government nationalized 245 Indian and foreign insurers and provident societies, leading to the formation of LIC through the enactment of the LIC Act, 1956, which received a capital contribution of Rs. 5 crores from the Indian government.

The General Insurance Sector in India

The roots of the general insurance sector in India can be traced back to the establishment of Triton Insurance Company Ltd., the inaugural general insurance company in 1850 in Calcutta by the British.

Significant milestones in the general insurance sector in India include:

1. **1907:** The establishment of Indian Mercantile Insurance Ltd., the first company to engage in all types of general insurance activities.
2. **1957:** The creation of the General Insurance Council, a division of the Insurance Association of India, which developed a code of conduct to ensure fair practices and sound business operations.
3. **1968:** The Insurance Act was amended to regulate investments, set minimum solvency requirements, and establish the Tariff Advisory Committee.
4. **1972:** The General Insurance Business (Nationalization) Act, 1972 led to the nationalization of the general insurance sector in India, with the transition date being 1st January 1973. 107 insurers were merged and organized into four entities: the National Insurance Company Ltd., the New India Assurance Company Ltd., the Oriental Insurance Company Ltd., and the United India Insurance Company Ltd. The General Insurance Corporation of India was also established.

1.6.2 Reforms in the Insurance Sector

In 1993, the Malhotra Committee, led by former Finance Secretary and RBI Governor R.N. Malhotra, was established to assess the Indian insurance sector and suggest its future direction.

The Malhotra Committee was created with the goal of enhancing the reforms initiated in the financial sector. These reforms aimed to develop a more efficient and competitive financial system that meets the economic needs, considering the ongoing structural changes and acknowledging the significance of insurance within the broader financial framework, necessitating similar reforms.

By 1994, the committee had submitted its report, which included several key recommendations:

a) Structure

- The government's stake in insurance companies should be reduced to 50%.
  - The government should acquire the shares of GIC and its subsidiaries, allowing these subsidiaries to operate independently.
  - Insurance companies should have more freedom in their operations.

b) Competition

- Private companies with a minimum capital of Rs. 1 billion should be permitted to enter the market.
  - No single entity should engage in both Life and General Insurance.
  - Foreign companies could be allowed to enter the market in partnership with local companies.
  - Postal Life Insurance should be permitted to serve rural areas.
  - Only one State-level Life Insurance Company should be authorized to operate in each state.

c) Regulatory Body

- The Insurance Act needed to be revised.
    - An Insurance Regulatory Authority should be established.
    - The Controller of Insurance (currently under the Finance Ministry) should gain independence.

d) Investments

- The mandatory investment of LIC Life Fund in government securities by the LIC should be lowered from 75% to 50%.
    - GIC and its subsidiaries should not exceed a 5% ownership in any company, with a plan to reduce their current holdings to this level over time.

e) Customer Service

- LIC should compensate for delays in payments beyond 30 days.
    - Insurance companies should be encouraged to introduce unit-linked pension plans.
    - The insurance industry needed to modernize its operations and technology.

The committee highlighted the importance of improving customer service and expanding insurance coverage through competition. However, it also stressed the need for caution to prevent any negative impact on public trust in the industry. Therefore, it recommended a cautious approach to competition by setting a minimum capital requirement of Rs. 100 crores. The committee proposed granting more independence to insurance companies to enhance their performance and economic motivations, suggesting the creation of an independent regulatory body.

1.6.3 Key Policy Reforms

The insurance industry has been opened to competition from private Indian companies following the enactment of the Insurance Regulatory and Development Authority Act, 1999 (IRDA Act). According to the IRDA Act, 1999, the Insurance Regulatory and Development Authority (IRDA) was created on April 19, 2000, with the aim of safeguarding the rights of policyholders and overseeing, encouraging, and ensuring the orderly expansion of the insurance sector. The IRDA Act 1999 facilitated the entry of private entities into the insurance market, which was previously dominated by public sector insurance companies and corporations. Under the new framework, private Indian insurance companies in the private sector were allowed to operate within India, subject to the following conditions:

1. The company is established and registered under the Companies Act, 1956;
2. The total equity shareholding by a foreign company, whether directly or indirectly through its subsidiaries or nominees, does not exceed 26%, and the equity capital of the Indian insurance company must be fully paid up;
3. The company's primary business activities are in life insurance, general insurance, or reinsurance;
4. The minimum fully paid-up equity capital required for life or general insurance activities is set at Rs.100 crores.
5. The minimum fully paid-up equity capital for reinsurance activities has been set at Rs.200 crores.

The Authority has issued 27 Regulations covering a range of topics, including the registration of insurers, regulations for insurance agents, solvency margin requirements, reinsurance regulations, obligations of insurers towards rural and social sectors, investment and accounting standards, and protection of policyholders' interests, among others. Applications for the issuance of the Certificate of Registration for both life and non-life insurers were opened by the Authority starting from August 15, 2000. The Authority's headquarters are located in Hyderabad.

1.6.4 Safeguarding the Interests of Policyholders:

The Insurance Regulatory and Development Authority (IRDA) bears the duty of safeguarding the interests of insurance policyholders. To fulfill this mandate, the Authority has implemented the following measures:

i.   The IRDA has promulgated the Protection of Policyholders Interest Regulations 2001, which stipulate the following: the provision of policy proposal documents in language that is easily comprehensible; the establishment of mechanisms for addressing grievances; the facilitation of the swift resolution of claims; and the provision of services to policyholders. Additionally, the Regulation mandates that insurers compensate policyholders for any delays in claim settlement.

ii. Insurers are obligated to maintain sufficient solvency margins to ensure they can fulfill their obligations to policyholders concerning claim payments.

iii. Insurance companies are required to clearly disclose the benefits, terms, and conditions of their policies. Advertisements issued by insurers must not mislead the public.

iv. All insurers are mandated to establish appropriate grievance redressal mechanisms at their headquarters and other branches.

v.   The Authority addresses any complaints received from policyholders regarding the services provided under their insurance contracts.

1.6.5 General Insurance Companies:

Private Sector Entities

i.   Aditya Birla Health Insurance Company Ltd.
ii.   Bajaj Allianz General Insurance Company Ltd.
iii.   Bharti AXA General Insurance Company Ltd.
iv.   Cholamandalam General Insurance Company Ltd.
v.   Future Generali India Insurance Company Ltd.
vi.   HDFC ERGO General Insurance Company Ltd.
vii.   ICICI Lombard General Insurance Company Ltd.
viii. IFFCO-Tokio General Insurance Company Ltd.
ix.   Kotak General Insurance Company Ltd.
x.   Liberty Videocon General Insurance Company Ltd.
xi.   Magma HDI General Insurance Company Ltd.
xii.   Raheja QBE General Insurance Company Ltd.
xiii. Reliance General Insurance Company Ltd.
xiv.   Royal Sundaram Alliance Insurance Company Ltd.
xv.   SBI General Insurance Company Ltd.
xvi.   Shriram General Insurance Company Ltd.
xvii. TATA AIG General Insurance Company Ltd.
xviii. Universal Sompo General Insurance Company Ltd.

1.6.6 Health Insurance Companies

1. Apollo Munich Health Insurance Company Ltd.
2. Star Health Allied Insurance Company Ltd.
3. Max Bupa Health Insurance Company Ltd.

4. Religare Health Insurance Company Ltd.
5. Cigna TTK Health Insurance Company Ltd.

This strategic partnership with international markets has significantly contributed to the growth of the Indian Insurance Sector, which now holds a substantial market share. In 2000, India permitted private entities to enter the insurance sector, setting a cap on Foreign Direct Investment (FDI) at 26%. This limit was increased to 49% in 2014.

The Insurance Laws (Amendment) Act, 2015 has further raised the Foreign Investment Cap in an Indian Insurance Company from 26% to an explicitly composite limit of 490/0, while ensuring the retention of Indian ownership and control. Private insurers such as HDFC, ICICI, and SBI have emerged as formidable competitors in offering life and non-life insurance products in India.

1.6.7 The Evolution of the Insurance Sector in India

While LIC remains the leading force in the Indian Insurance sector, the emergence of new private insurers is set to spark a dynamic expansion and growth across both life and non-life sectors in 2017. The demand for affordable insurance policies is at an all-time high. Given the domestic economy's limited potential for significant growth, the Indian insurance sector is poised for robust expansion. With rising incomes and a substantial increase in purchasing power, along with higher household savings, the Indian insurance sector is poised to adopt new trends such as product innovation, multi-channel distribution, improved claims management, and regulatory trends in the Indian market.

The government is also making concerted efforts to provide insurance coverage to individuals living below the poverty line through various schemes, including:
- Pradhan Mantri Suraksha Bima Yojana (PMSBY),
- Rashtriya Swasthya Bima Yojana (RSBY), and
- Pradhan Mantri Jeevan Jyoti Bima Yojana (PMJJBY).

The introduction of these schemes is expected to enable individuals from lower and lower-middle-income groups to access insurance policies at lower premiums in India.

With numerous regulatory changes taking place in the Indian insurance sector, the future appears bright and promising for the life insurance sector. This will lead to a transformation in how insurers manage their operations and interact with their genuine customers.

Factors such as the increasing insurance awareness among the population, the importance of retirement planning, the growth of the middle class, and the rise in the number of young individuals who are insurable are expected to significantly boost the growth of the insurance sector in India.

1.6.8 Global Insurance Market Overview

On a worldwide scale, the insurance sector saw a significant increase in premium revenues in 2015, rising by 5.6 percent, in contrast, the anticipated growth rate for 2016 is set to be notably lower, at 4.4 percent. The total amount of premiums is set to climb to €4.6 trillion, marking an increase from the previous year's total of €4.4 trillion.

What are the key reasons behind the industry's performance? The global insurance sector is currently navigating through turbulent times, influenced by factors such as the ongoing low interest rate environment, a challenging stock market, and regulatory changes, including the US Department of Labor (DOL) rule and new tax regulations. Meanwhile, there has been a shift among consumers towards a combination of online and offline research and purchasing, with this trend reaching its peak in developed countries and gaining momentum in developing nations, driven by the proliferation of mobile phones. These shifts, coupled with the impact of price comparison websites, technological advancements, and the push towards digitalization, are major forces compelling insurers to adapt their business strategies.

In developed markets in North America and Western Europe, insurers have had to exert considerable effort to adapt to these trends. With life premiums decreasing and property and casualty premiums becoming more stable, these developed markets have shown slower growth compared to emerging markets, and our report begins to highlight these significant disparities by business segment and geographical area.

Specifically, preliminary data for business segments globally indicates that health insurance experienced the highest growth rate from 2015 to 2016, followed by property and casualty insurance at 4.2 percent, while life insurance saw a decline in its growth rate of gross written premiums (GWP) from 4.8 percent in 2015 to 3.8 percent in 2016.

Regionally, Europe, Middle East, and Africa (EMEA) has seen moderate growth in both property and casualty and health insurance sectors, whereas life insurance is expected to see a decrease. The Americas region has shown strong growth in health and moderate growth in property and casualty insurance, with life insurance anticipated to be volatile due to changes in US regulations, and is projected to end 2016 with a slight decline in the Americas as a whole. In Asia-Pacific, the insurance industry has expanded across all three segments, with health insurance experiencing double-digit growth.

In terms of business segments, initial findings indicate several significant trends:

Across most regions, except for the Americas and Western Europe, there was a positive trend in life growth during 2016. However, the extent of this growth and the reasons behind it varied by region. A notable shift from the previous year, Asian nations like China, Hong Kong (treated as a separate entity), and India led the way in terms of the strongest increases. Among life products, endowments saw the most significant growth, primarily driven by emerging Asia and the United States, while Unit-linked (UL) products experienced a decline in the United States and Western Europe. The key financial metric for life, life return on equity (ROE), rose from 11 percent in 2014 to 11.8 percent in 2015, and it's anticipated to remain at or below 10 percent moving forward.

Over the last five years, the global insurance sector has maintained stability, growing at a consistent rate of 5 percent. It's also projected to increase by 4.2 percent in 2016, expanding the global P&C market to €1.39 trillion. Regionally, while the Asia-Pacific (APAC) region, which accounts for just 23 percent of the total market, has been the primary catalyst for growth, growing at an average rate of 9 percent per year since 2013, and is expected to accelerate further. Conversely, the Americas and the European Middle East and Africa (EMEA) regions, which together make up 49 percent and 29 percent of the global market, are anticipated to grow at a modest rate of 2 to 3 percent over the next two years. Looking ahead, we expect to see a decline in growth, or even negative growth, in mature markets due to factors like safer vehicles and increased technology for risk mitigation in homes and factories.

The distribution landscape for insurance products and regions varies. In life insurance, bancassurance is the dominant distribution model in many Asian and European areas, while brokers are more favoured in North America. For property and casualty insurance, agents and brokers still lead, but there's a noticeable rise in the use of direct distribution methods across various regions. Studies of direct distribution companies in some areas show they're outperforming their markets. Direct distribution will play a crucial role in addressing the challenge of cost reduction, especially with the rise of digital disruptors and price comparison websites. While direct distribution is showing signs of slowing down in Western Europe, the shift towards hybrid models, where customers are more price-conscious, means there's increased pressure on costs and a need for a complete transformation of non-direct operations to fully embrace multi- or omnichannel strategies. Companies looking for the most promising growth opportunities in the global insurance markets should consider both the fastest-growing and the largest developed markets. However, the slowing growth rates suggest that most insurers will need to look beyond their current markets for new opportunities.

1.7 Handling Risk by Individuals and Insurance Companies

The process of managing risk involves assessing and quantifying the likelihood and financial impact of potential events that could occur in a customer's environment, which may necessitate a payout by the insurer. It also includes the ability to distribute the risk associated with these events among other insurance companies in the market. The work of risk management often includes the use of mathematical and statistical models to determine the appropriate level of insurance coverage and the value of the insurance risk in terms of 'holding' vs 'distributing'.

Risk = Probability x Severity

Risk is defined as the product of the probability of an event happening and the severity of the resulting loss.

Speculative Risk: This type of risk involves outcomes that could be either a loss, a profit, or no change at all. Examples include investments in the stock market and decisions related to launching new products, opening new locations, etc.

Pure Risk: This type of risk is characterized by outcomes that are either a loss or no loss at all. This includes scenarios like property damage from a fire, theft from a building, accidents involving employees, etc.

Steps for Implementing Risk Management:

a. **Quantify and Rank:** One method for this is through risk mapping. Essentially, you plot all identified risks on a map, which highlights which risks require your attention. Collaborate with your broker to ensure you have coverage for all relevant risks and seek ways to prevent and reduce these risks. The image on the right shows a typical risk map. However, risk maps are often customized to meet the specific needs of the organization.
b. **Identify Risks:** It's beneficial to organize risks in a manner that allows for the identification of the most common and significant risks, enabling you to allocate resources effectively.
c. **Embrace Risk Sensitivity, Not Risk Aversion:** Being sensitive to risk doesn't equate to being overly cautious. It's important to recognize that risks are inherent in every aspect of life. Approach risk management with a deliberate and systematic strategy, while maintaining a realistic perspective.
d. **Identify Risks in Business Decisions:** The approach to identifying risks in business decisions is similar to that of any other risk. The key is to be thorough and utilize all available resources. These risks can be prioritized and mapped in the same manner as other risks.

Issues with Products or Services

When customers feel that a product or service did not meet their expectations, challenges and risks naturally arise.

Options for Mitigating Product or Service Issues:

a. Integrate ERM software into your organization to minimize negligence claims.
b. Invest in professional liability insurance.
c. Perform thorough vendor due diligence to prevent third-party providers from delivering products or services that fall short of your organization's standards.

Damage of Property

Insurance firms frequently focus on safeguarding their clients' tangible assets, including both physical buildings and land. Although natural disasters and other incidents might not completely destroy property, they always present a significant risk to a business's ability to function normally.

Options for Reducing Risks:

a. Put in place measures to reduce and prevent risks.

b.   Purchase sufficient insurance coverage.

c.   Create a reliable plan for continuing business operations that is actively shared with all employees.

1.8 Adjusting Insurance Premiums

Fundamental Components in Calculating Insurance Premiums

In essence, the cost of your life insurance premium is made up of four main components:

a.   Mortality charge ("natural premium")

b.   Expense component

c.   Investment component

d.   Emergency reserve

a. Mortality

Life insurance operates on an actuarial basis that considers the likelihood of death at certain ages or groups of ages. In simpler terms, it's understood that older individuals are more likely to pass away. This concept applies to life insurance as well. The older someone is, the higher the chance of their death. Other factors such as health, job, lifestyle, and hobbies can also significantly impact the chance of early death. All these factors contribute to the mortality aspect of an insurance company's life insurance premium.

To simplify things, insurance companies use mortality tables created by actuaries. These tables provide information on the likelihood of a person dying before their next birthday based on their age. Using this table, an insurance company can estimate the chance of someone living to a certain age and the expected lifespan of individuals at various ages. The premium calculated from the mortality table is known as the "natural premium," which is the primary and largest part of the total premium a policyholder pays.

Initially, life insurance was operated by mutual societies based on guilds. A bookseller named John Hartley initiated one of these societies in London in 1705, limiting membership to those aged between 12 and 45. Under Hartley's system, all members paid the same premium, and at the end of the year, the funds were distributed among the dependents of members who passed away that year. Two years after the start of the society, it began offering a fixed benefit of £ 125 to each member.

During one of my talks, a gentleman expressed his desire to speak, and I asked him to proceed. While he was speaking, he mistakenly referred to me as an "Undertaker." Of course, I had to correct him, explaining that we are "Underwriters," not "Undertakers." However, the gentleman might not be entirely mistaken when looking into the history of mortality tables further.

James Dodson, a math teacher, was turned away from John Hartley's program because he was 46, a year over the age limit. Consequently, Dodson, being a mathematician, resorted to studying death rates in graveyards to create a mortality table. This table recorded the number of deaths at various ages from 1756 to 1759, marking the first scientifically constructed mortality table. Dodson's table allowed each member to pay a set premium amount until their death, at which point the beneficiaries would receive a payout.

b. Costs

The cost of your premium also includes a portion for the expenses the insurance company incurs in processing your policy. These costs cover the commission paid to the agent who sold you the policy, the printing costs of your policy document, and other overhead expenses of the insurance company. However, don't be concerned. Since there are thousands or millions of others purchasing the same insurance product, these costs are spread thin, minimizing their impact on the total premium you pay as an individual. This is why you often don't notice this aspect when calculating your premium. Yet, it's there. This situation further supports the fundamental principle of the "Law of Large Numbers" in life insurance.

c. Investment

This part can be referred to as the "Savings element," "Investment element," or "Profit element." You're correct in calling it any of these. The premium you pay includes a percentage for investment. This amount is invested by the company, and it's from these investments that bonuses, cash values, and policy loans are distributed to policyholders of permanent life policies. It's important to note that this statement assumes the investment element is only included in the premiums for permanent policies (such as endowment and whole life). While this is generally true, it's not entirely accurate. Regardless of the policy type, an insurance company expects to earn a profit as a business. Therefore, the investment aspect of a life insurance premium includes an allowance for the expected moderate profit of a life office. This is similar to how a manufacturer would add a profit margin to the cost of their product.

d. Contingencies

What happens if the assumptions of a life office don't pan out? What if, instead of the expected 20 policyholders passing away in a year, the company experiences 200 deaths? What if a major economic downturn negatively affects the company's investments? What if the company initially overestimated the number of potential buyers of its product? What if the cost of doing business for the company doubles unexpectedly? What if...? We can continue to list various scenarios that could disrupt the calculations of a life office.

1.9 Re-Insurance

1.9.1 Reinsurance for Insurance Companies

Reinsurance involves an insurance company choosing to insure a significant risk itself, then transferring the excess risk to a reinsurance company or multiple companies to spread the risk out. This is done to share the financial risk.

Should a claim be filed by the insured, the insurance company is responsible for covering the insured's losses if the claim meets the policy's terms and conditions. This places a financial burden on the insurance company.

To mitigate this risk, insurance companies also insure themselves against such financial burdens. They do this by entering into agreements with reinsurance companies, also known as third-party reinsurers.

The reinsurance agreement between an insurance company and a reinsurance company is called reinsurance. This agreement stipulates that the reinsurance company will compensate the insurance company for any losses incurred by the insurance company when it pays out on the original contract.

Reinsurance protection is only available after the insurance company has paid out a claim. In essence, this means that the insurance company must first settle the claim and then seek reimbursement from the reinsurance company.

This process is akin to seeking indemnity for losses, which only becomes effective once the insurance company has settled a claim and paid the original policyholder.

Thus, insurance companies can transfer their losses to reinsurance companies through reinsurance contracts. In return, reinsurance companies benefit by diversifying their own risks, as they ensure that the insured must reduce their reserve requirements, thereby increasing their assets.

1.9.2 Re-insured Parties:

Every insurance policy involves two main parties: the insurer and the insured. However, in the case of re-insurance, a third party, known as the re-insurer, is introduced. This re-insurer steps in to provide additional coverage for the risks associated with the policy. The insurer, which initially issued the policy to the policyholder, then reinsures it with the re-insurer to ensure it is adequately protected.

The policyholder, whether it's for life, property, or any other type of insurance, is reinsured by their original insurer without their knowledge. As a result, the policyholder has no direct rights against the reinsurance company.

The original insurance policy is the foundational document for any reinsurance agreement. For reinsurance to be valid, the policy must be for a specific interest that outlines the involved parties' interests. These specific interests are essential for securing a reinsurance policy.

Once a reinsurance policy is in place, these interests cannot be changed. The reinsurance amount and duration cannot exceed what was initially specified in the reinsurance policy, and the reinsurance policy cannot extend beyond the original policy's term.

Re-insured parties can choose from several types of reinsurance:

a. Facultative Re-insurance:

This type of reinsurance, also known as optional policies, is issued at the discretion of the reinsurance company. These policies are issued based on a case-by-case analysis of the policy's circumstances and facts. The coverage provided by these policies can vary, ranging from full to partial coverage, depending on the policy's risk level. These policies are designed to mitigate the risk associated with specific policies.

b. Treaty Re-insurance:

This is a unique type of reinsurance policy issued by the reinsured. Treaty policies are akin to agreements or negotiations, such as treaties. They typically involve a written agreement to ensure a specific category of policies issued by the reinsured. This category could be all property insurance policies, accident, or other types of casualty insurance policies. A key aspect of treaty insurance is that it transfers the risk to the insurer for all policies covered by the treaty, not just one specific policy.

c. Double Insurance:

This refers to a situation where the insured benefits from two overlapping policies, each covering the same risk from two different insurance companies. In the event of a claim, the insured can seek compensation from both insurance companies. However, it's important to note that the insured cannot receive more than the actual losses or damages suffered.

Insurance companies are legally obligated to distribute only the genuine losses in the same ratio as they divide the total premium. For instance, if someone purchases an insurance policy for a loss of Rs. 100.00 from company (A) and then again for the same amount from company (B), and the total loss amounts to Rs. 150.00.

The person insured cannot claim Rs. 100.00 from both companies, aiming to aggregate the insurance payout to Rs. 200.00 and to earn a profit of Rs. 50.00. Instead, both companies are responsible for sharing the risk based on the premiums paid to each.

d. Duplicate Insurance:

There's often confusion between duplicate insurance and duplicate coverage. Duplicate coverage occurs when two insurance companies deal with the same person and agree to cover that individual against the same risks.

When a person has duplicate insurance, they are covered by two different insurance companies for the same interest and subject matter. For example, if a husband and wife each have duplicate medical insurance that covers the other, they would, therefore, have duplicate insurance.

It's rare for an individual to collect on duplicate insurance, as this would typically be seen as a form of Unjust Enrichment, and many insurance contracts have clauses that prevent this.

e. Co-insurance:

Co-insurance is less common in India, but it's defined by the sharing of co-pays between the insured and the insurer. In simpler terms, it's an insurance where the risk is shared between the insurer and the insured. This arrangement helps to lower the insured's premium costs and benefits others insured within the same group.

The terms and conditions of co-insurance can be complex because they often overlap or contradict each other. Therefore, it's crucial to fully understand the terms before choosing co-insurance. In essence, co-insurance is an insurance where the risk is shared between the insurer and the insured, similar to co-pay.

In broad strokes, there's an agreement between the insurance company and the policyholder that stipulates the policyholder is responsible for covering a certain percentage of the costs after deductibles, with the remaining amount to be paid by the insurance company. This arrangement is known as co-insurance, which essentially means that the policyholder and the insurance company share the financial burden of the costs.

Within the realm of co-insurance, two key terms are often mentioned: Co-Pay and Deductibles. It's important for every policyholder to understand the difference between these two terms. Co-Pay refers to a fixed amount that the policyholder is expected to pay at the time of each doctor's visit. It's important to note that this is not a percentage of the doctor's fees. Depending on the policy's terms and conditions, the policyholder may be required to cover both the co-insurance and the co-pay for doctor's visits.

1.10 The Importance of Insurance in Economic Progress and Social Protection

Our world is brimming with uncertainties and dangers. People, families, companies, properties, and assets face various kinds and degrees of risks, including the potential for loss of life, health, possessions, and property. Although it's not always feasible to prevent these negative events from happening, the financial sector has developed solutions to shield individuals and businesses from these losses by offering financial backing. Insurance is a financial tool that lowers or removes the financial burden of losses caused by various risks.

In addition to safeguarding individuals and businesses from numerous potential threats, the insurance industry plays a vital role in the overall economic advancement of a country by ensuring the stability of business operations and providing long-term financial support for industrial projects. The insurance industry also fosters the habit of saving among individuals and creates jobs for millions, particularly in countries like India where saving and employment are crucial.

Shifts Risk: Insurance allows for the transfer of the risk of loss from the insured to the insurer. The fundamental idea behind insurance is to distribute the risk among a large group of people. A wide array of individuals acquires insurance policies and pay their premiums to the insurer. Whenever a loss occurs, the insurer compensates for it using the funds collected from the millions of policyholders.

Boosts Economic Development: The insurance sector significantly influences the overall economy by mobilizing domestic savings. It transforms accumulated capital into productive investments. Insurance also helps in reducing losses, ensuring financial stability, and promoting trade and commerce activities, which in turn leads to sustainable economic growth and development. Therefore, insurance is essential for the sustainable growth of an economy.

Offers Protection and Security to Individuals and Businesses: Insurance provides financial backing and diminishes the uncertainties that individuals and businesses encounter throughout their lifecycles. It offers a reliable risk management strategy against events that could potentially cause financial hardship to individuals and businesses. For example, with the rising cost of medical care at around 15% annually, even basic medical treatments can disrupt a family's carefully planned budget. However, having health insurance ensures financial protection for the family. For businesses, insurance provides financial compensation for losses due to fire, theft, accidents related to maritime activities, and other incidents.

Offers Assistance to Families in Health Crises: The welfare of a family is crucial for everyone, with the health of its members being a primary concern for many. Whether it's the elderly parents or the newborns, the need for medication and hospital stays is significant in maintaining family well-being. The escalating costs of medical treatments and the high prices of drugs can quickly deplete your savings if you're not adequately prepared. Anyone can suddenly face severe health issues like heart attacks, strokes, or cancer. Moreover, the increasing cost of medical care is a major worry. Health Insurance is a policy that safeguards individuals financially against various health risks. With this insurance, policyholders receive financial aid during medical emergencies.

Creates Sustainable Financial Assets: The Insurance industry generates revenue through premiums collected from millions of policyholders. These funds are long-term, which leads to their investment in infrastructure projects like roads, ports, power plants, dams, etc., crucial for the development of a nation. These large investments also boost employment, leading to an increase in capital within the economy.

1.11. Components of the Insurance Industry

The insurance industry has grown from its inception with the first car insurance policy to the diverse range of life insurance offerings available today. This industry is structured to include property and casualty insurers, life insurers, and health insurers. Each of these categories is subject to specific regulations regarding their policies. The industry is governed by a mix of state and federal regulations, contingent upon the nature of the insurance provided.

Cooperative Ownership

A significant number of insurance companies are part of a cooperative structure, where a single corporation owns one or more insurance entities that operate autonomously. The most prevalent form of cooperative ownership for an insurance company is through a captive insurer. This entity is established to cover a variety of business risks, with reinsurance being the most common service provided. Reinsurance involves multiple insurance companies sharing the burden of losses.

Cooperative Insurance Companies

A cooperative insurance company is owned by its policyholders, granting each policyholder a vote in the selection of board members. These companies can offer a wide array of insurance products or focus on a single type of coverage for their clients. The profits generated by these companies are returned to the policyholders in the form of dividends.

Health Insurance

The insurance sector also encompasses companies that provide health insurance to individuals and employers through group health insurance policies. Companies that offer group health insurance to employers are subject to a blend of federal and state regulations. Additionally, states may offer health insurance to residents if it is not available from private insurers due to financial constraints or ineligibility.

Life Insurance

Life insurers, a subset of property and casualty insurers, also provide life insurance products. These insurers can be mutual, owned by their policyholders, or part of a stock insurer, owned by shareholders. Life insurers typically offer financial products to their policyholders, including annuities and certain mutual funds.

Stock Insurers

A stock insurer is owned by its shareholders, with a focus on both protecting the policyholders and maximizing profits for the shareholders. While stock insurers may distribute profits to shareholders in the form of dividends, they generally do not allocate dividends to their policyholders.

Property and Casualty Insurers

Property and casualty insurers provide a variety of insurance products to individuals, including automobile and homeowners' insurance. These insurers also offer commercial insurance solutions for businesses, such as small business packages, general business liability, umbrella policies, and workers' compensation. The regulation of these insurers varies by state where they issue policies.

1.12 Functions of Insurance Companies

The primary functions of insurance companies include:

a. Determining Premiums
b. Assessing Risk
c. Generating Revenue
d. Handling Claims
e. Collaborating with Reinsurers

Insurance companies also undertake additional activities such as financial management, legal services, risk mitigation, and information technology.

Determining Premiums

a. Determining premiums involves calculating the cost of insurance based on actuarial analysis.
b. In life insurance, actuaries set the cost of life and health insurance policies and annuities, which also determine the legal reserves required by the company for future liabilities.
c. In property and casualty insurance, actuaries also set the rates for various insurance policies and assess the adequacy of loss reserves, allocate costs, and gather data for management and regulatory purposes.

Assessing Risk

a. Risk is measured in terms of exposure units, which vary by type of insurance.
b. The individual responsible for assessing risk and setting premiums is known as an actuary. Actuaries are highly skilled mathematicians who are involved in every aspect of insurance company operations, from planning to pricing to research.

Generating Revenue

a. Generating revenue involves the collection of premiums and the management of investments.
b. Premiums are the amount paid by the insured for coverage.
c. Investments are managed to ensure the company's financial stability and growth.

Handling Claims

a. Claims handling includes the processing of insurance claims from policyholders.
b. Claims are evaluated based on the terms of the policy and the severity of the loss.
c. Claims are settled by either the insurance company or the policyholder, depending on the policy's terms.

Collaborating with Reinsurers

a. Reinsurance involves sharing the risk of insurance policies with another company.
b. Reinsurers provide financial protection to insurance companies by sharing in the risk of policyholders.
c. This collaboration helps insurance companies manage their risk exposure and financial stability.

1.12.1 Insurance Service Operations services

Enhancing the operating model: This involves analyzing the company's processes, technology, and organizational structure, as well as its performance management, in comparison to other insurers and its own strategic objectives. The goal is to transform the operating model by moving away from fixed costs to variable ones, eliminating processes and technologies that do not add value, and focusing more on growth, distribution, and product innovation.

Optimizing outdated processes and technologies: This step is about finding ways to better serve customers, boost employee satisfaction, and increase cost efficiency by updating policy administration systems and other technologies, making processes more streamlined, and ensuring a seamless customer experience across different product lines and distribution channels.

Benchmarking carrier performance: This involves assessing how well the carrier performs compared to industry leaders to pinpoint areas for potential operational improvements and enhancements in customer service quality while keeping costs in check.

Better management of policyholder relationships: This includes using data and analytical tools to support cross-selling and upselling efforts, improving customer retention, and enhancing the ability to select risks effectively.

Strategic underwriting: This is about assisting insurers in building profitable relationships with customers by making more accurate risk assessments and making sound underwriting decisions that balance risk and pricing. It also involves identifying new customer segments that are both profitable and high-risk using predictive tools and analytical models.

Reducing the cost of claims: This includes making the claims process more efficient and automated, finding ways to predict potential claim losses, improving the management of third-party suppliers, enhancing the process for handling litigation, and using advanced fraud detection methods to reduce losses.

Managing enterprise costs: This is about developing long-term, cost-effective strategies for managing resources that align with the company's strategic objectives. It also includes efforts to refine processes, simplify the organization, rationalize infrastructure, and improve how spend is managed.

Potential financial advantages include:
- Increased profitability

- Reduction in operating expenses by up to 20 percent
- Enhanced process standardization and compliance
- Improved reliability and accuracy of systems
- Reduction in underwriting loss ratios by up to 7 points over a period of 18 to 24 months
- Lowering of claims costs through better claims management
- Improved reliability and accuracy of systems
- Better customer experience for both policyholders and distribution partners
- Greater adaptability to changing customer demands

1.12.2 Rules for Insurance Agents

An Insurance Agent is a person or a company that acts as a middleman between the customer and the insurance provider. This includes both individual agents and corporate agents, which can be banks or brokers. Additionally, it encompasses Surveyors and Third-Party Administrators, although these entities are not directly involved in acquiring business. Surveyors evaluate losses on behalf of the insurance companies, while Third-Party Administrators offer services related to health insurance for insurance companies.

On September 2, 2019, the Department of Financial Services made certain changes to the Indian Insurance Companies (Foreign Investment) Rules, 2015, allowing 100% foreign investment in insurance intermediaries (such as Third-Party Administrators, web aggregators, insurance brokers, etc.), as long as they are approved by the Insurance Regulatory and Development Authority of India (CIRDAI) and adhere to the pricing guidelines set by the Reserve Bank of India (RBI). On October 30, 2019, the Insurance Regulatory and Development Authority of India updated various rules applicable to insurance intermediaries by introducing the IRDAI (Insurance Intermediaries) (Amendment) Regulations, 2019 (Intermediaries Amendment Regulations') for the following purposes:

- Mandating that the chairman of the board or the managing director/chief executive officer/principal officer of an insurance intermediary must be a citizen of India.

- Requiring prior approval from the IRDAI for the return of dividends.

- Prohibiting insurance intermediaries from making payments (except dividends) to related parties, in total, exceeding 10% of the total expenses for the fiscal year.

- Requiring that at least half of the directors and key management personnel be Indian citizens.

Insurance is a complex product that guarantees compensation to the insured or a third party according to specific terms and conditions in the event of a covered event. In most insurance transactions, there is an intermediary, which can be an insurance agent (either individual or corporate) or an insurance broker.

- Insurance intermediaries act as a conduit between consumers (looking to purchase insurance policies) and insurance companies (seeking to sell those policies).
- Insurance brokers are authorized by the IRDA and are regulated by the Insurance Regulatory and Development Authority (Insurance Brokers) Regulations, 2002. Individual insurance agents and corporate agents are also authorized by the IRDA and are regulated by the Insurance Regulatory and Development Authority (Licensing of Individual Insurance Agents) Regulations, 2000 and the Insurance Regulatory and Development Authority (Licensing of Corporate Agents) Regulations, 2002, respectively. These regulations outline the Code of Conduct for these intermediaries.

No intermediary is allowed to offer any discounts to you to encourage you to purchase the policy. If any such inducement is made, it breaches Section 41 of the Insurance Act, 1938, and all parties involved could face legal action as stipulated by the law.

Considering the information provided, the Insurance Regulatory and Development Authority of India (IRDAI) issued a supplementary circular on November 19, 2019, following the withdrawal of the guidelines from November 20, 2015, on 'Indian owned and controlled' for insurance intermediaries. Additionally, there are notifications pending for the implementation of 100% foreign equity investment in insurance intermediaries under exchange control regulations.

The Insurance Regulatory and Development Authority's Consumer Affairs Department has launched the Integrated Grievance Management System (IGMS), an online platform for registering and monitoring grievances. It is mandatory to lodge a grievance with the insurance company first. Should you be dissatisfied with the company's resolution, you can escalate the issue to IRDA through IGMS by visiting www.igms.irda.gov.in. For those unable to directly access the insurer's grievance system, IGMS also offers a gateway for grievance registration with the insurer.

In addition to registering grievances online through IGMS, there are several other methods available for grievance registration, including email (complaints@irda.gov.in), letter (address it to Consumer Affairs Department, Insurance Regulatory and Development Authority, 3rd Floor, Parishram Bhavan, Basheer Bagh, Hyderabad:4), or by calling the IRDA Call Centre at Toll Free 155255. The IRDA will register your complaint against insurance companies for free and assist in tracking its progress. The Call Centre can also help in filing complaints directly with insurance companies by providing details such as the company's address, telephone number, website, contact number, and email address. The Call Centre serves as a comprehensive alternative for customers and policyholders, offering round-the-clock tele-functionalities from 8 AM to 8 PM, Monday to Saturday, in Hindi, English, and various Indian languages.

Upon receiving a complaint, IRDA facilitates its resolution by engaging with the insurance company. The company is given a 15-day period to address the complaint. Should further investigation or inquiries be necessary, IRDA will conduct them. Moreover, IRDA advises the complainant to seek assistance from the Insurance Ombudsman in accordance with the Redressal of Public Grievances Rules, 1998.

1.12.3 Insurance Web Aggregators

Definitions:

a. "Act" refers to the Insurance Act, 1938 (4 of 1938), which has been amended over time. "Agreement" in this context signifies the contract between a web aggregator and an insurance company;

b. "Authority" is the Insurance Regulatory and Development Authority, established by Section 3 of the Insurance Regulatory and Development Authority Act, 1999 (41 of 1999);

c. "Distance Marketing" is the method of soliciting or selling insurance products or services when the customer is not physically present at the time of the sale, and this is done through telephone, Short Messaging Service (SMS), email, internet, or web services;

d. "Lead" is any information about a person who has visited a web aggregator's website and has provided contact details for the purpose of obtaining information on insurance product prices or features/benefits;

e. "Lead Generation" is the process of gathering information about potential customers to determine their interest in purchasing insurance before starting the sales process;

f. "Lead Management System" (LMS) is the software used by the web aggregator to manage, filter, validate, grade, distribute, follow up, and close leads from inquiries received on its website;

g. "Outsourcing" means the activities that a web aggregator can perform to the extent specified by the Authority.

"Person" includes:

a. A corporation registered under the Companies Act, 1956 (1 of 1956);

b. A limited liability partnership registered under the Limited Liability Partnership Act, 2008 (6 of 2009) with no partner being a non-resident entity or person living outside India as defined in clause (w) of section 2 of the Foreign Exchange Management Act, 1999 (42 of 1999), and not being a foreign limited liability partnership registered there;

c. Any other individual recognized by the Authority to act as a Web Aggregator.

"Principal Officer" refers to:

- A director or partner who oversees the operations of a Web Aggregator within a corporate structure; or

- The head of the Web Aggregator appointed specifically to manage its functions.

- "Solicitation" as per these Regulations is described as the process by which an insurer or intermediary attempts to persuade a potential customer to buy an insurance policy.

- "Tele caller" in this context is an individual hired by a Telemarketer to perform tasks related to Telemarketing and Distance Marketing.

- "Telemarketer" is defined as an organization that is registered with the Telecom Regulatory Authority of India under Chapter Ill of The Telecom Commercial Communications Customer Preference Regulations, 2010 (which have been amended over time).

- "Web Aggregator" is a person who has received a license from the Authority to operate under these Regulations.

- "Website" is a collection of related web pages hosted on a single domain. This website is served from at least one web server and can be accessed through a network like the Internet or a private local area network, identified by a Uniform resource locator. The term "website" also includes a web portal and/or a mobile application for the purposes of these Regulations.

- "Designated Website" is a website(s) with a domain name(s) that are registered, owned, and exclusively utilized by the Web Aggregator for its operations.

Words and terms not explicitly defined in these Regulations but are covered by the Insurance Act, 1938 (4 of 1938), the Insurance Regulatory and Development Authority Act, 1999, or any of the Regulations made under these Acts will be given their respective definitions under those Acts.

1.12.4 Requirements for Web Aggregator License:

i. To obtain or renew a web aggregator license, the applicant must meet the following criteria:

ii. The applicant must be an individual as defined in section 1 (i).

iii. The company or any other documents submitted by the applicant must exclusively focus on the web aggregation of insurance products.

iv. The applicant should not be involved in any other business activities besides the primary focus of web aggregation of insurance products.

v. The applicant is prohibited from being licensed or registered under any insurance intermediary roles, such as insurance agent, corporate agent, micro-insurance agent, TPA, surveyor, loss assessor, or any other insurance intermediary roles as per the applicable regulations.

vi. The applicant is not allowed to have any referral agreements with insurance companies.

The applicant must not have any business relationships with insurance companies, insurance brokers, corporate agents, micro-insurance agents, TPA, surveyors, loss assessors, or any other insurance intermediaries at any point.

i. The main officer of the web aggregator must hold the necessary qualifications as outlined by the regulatory body.

ii. The main officer of the web aggregator is required to complete an initial 50 hours of training and 25 hours of refresher training every three years.

iii. The main officer, along with the directors, promoters, shareholders, partners, key management, and other key personnel, must meet the criteria set by the Financial Inclusion and Protection (FIT) and Property Rights (PROPER) guidelines as issued by the authority.

iv. The web aggregator must not have breached any obligations or the regulatory code of conduct.

v. The regulatory authority believes that granting the license will benefit the policyholders.

1.12.5. Application for License as Web Aggregator

i. An individual or entity interested in obtaining a license as a Web Aggregator is required to submit an application to the designated authority using the provided application form.

ii. The application must include a non-refundable fee of ten thousand rupees, which should be paid using a bank draft drawn against the Insurance Regulatory and Development Authority and should be made payable to the Hyderabad office.

iii. Applicants who wish to engage in Outsourcing and Telemarketing activities should clearly indicate this intention in their application.

iv. To be granted a license as a Web Aggregator, the applicant must meet all the specified eligibility criteria and adhere to the conditions outlined in the regulations.

v. The authority will process the application for a Web Aggregator license in accordance with the relevant provisions and these regulations.

vi. Should the applicant satisfy all the eligibility criteria and requirements, the authority will issue a license allowing them to operate as a Web aggregator.

vii. A license issued will be valid for three years from the date of issuance, unless it is suspended or revoked under these regulations.

viii. An application that does not fully meet all the requirements will be rejected.

ix. Application for License Renewal:

x. Web Aggregators wishing to continue their operations are required to apply for license renewal at least thirty days prior to the expiration of their current license. The renewal application must include a fee of ten thousand rupees. Applicants interested in continuing their outsourcing and telemarketing activities should clearly state this in their application.

xi. A Web Aggregator will not be permitted to engage in their web aggregator functions after the license has expired.

The authority will process the renewal application for a Web Aggregator license in accordance with the applicable provisions and these regulations.

i. Before applying for license renewal, a Web Aggregator must ensure that their Principal Officer has completed at least twenty-five hours of theoretical and practical training from an institution recognized by the Authority at regular intervals.

ii. Upon being satisfied that the applicant meets all the renewal license conditions, the Authority will extend the license for a period of three years and notify the applicant of this decision.

iii. Should it be discovered that the Web Aggregator has not conducted any business activities during any part of the previous licensed period, the Authority may choose not to renew the license.

iv. Workers at the Web Aggregator: Workers at the Web Aggregator who are involved in the process of seeking out and checking insurance should have finished a total of fifty hours of both theory and hands-on training from a recognized institution at regular intervals and have successfully completed an exam at the conclusion of this training. This exam was held by the National Insurance Academy in Pune or any other approved testing body.

v. Web Aggregators that use tele-callers to pitch their services must ensure these callers are on the company's payroll and have received the necessary training approved by the Authority.

vi. The Web Aggregators are accountable for any actions or failures to act by their employees who are working on their behalf.

1.12.6 Requirements for Web Aggregators

- 1956. The web aggregator's capital must be issued and subscribed in the form of Equity a at all times.
- 1958. The web aggregator must submit a certificate of net worth, certified by a Chartered Accountant, to the Authority annually following the completion of the financial year.

1.12.7 Responsibilities and Responsibilities of Web Aggregators

a) The web aggregator is obligated to:

i. Display details about insurers who have entered into agreements with the web aggregator.

ii. Perform activities aimed at generating leads for insurers.

iii. Ensure that the information systems, including both hardware and software, such as aggregation websites, lead management systems, and data centres hosting these systems, adhere to the current information security standards and procedures in India.

iv. Transmit leads and other data to insurers using secure data encryption technologies, such as 128-bit encryption.

v. Utilize only payment gateways licensed by the Reserve Bank of India for premium collection and transfer to insurers when authorized by the insurer to handle premium collection on their behalf.

vi. Maintain the information systems (both hardware and software) including aggregation websites, lead management systems, and data centers hosting these systems, through audits by CERT-In, an accredited information security auditing organization, at least once a year. A copy of the audit certificate or report must be submitted to IRDA and the insurers with whom the web aggregator has a contract, within 15 days of receiving the certificate or report.

b) The web aggregator is prohibited from:

i. Displaying information related to the products or services of other financial institutions, FMCG companies, or any other product or service on their website.

ii. Displaying any form of advertising, including for products or services, including insurance products or services, other financial products or services, or any other product or service on their website.

iii. Operating multiple websites or forming partnerships with entities that are either approved, unapproved, or unlicensed for lead generation or product comparison.

iv. Operating websites of other financial, commercial, marketing, sales, or service entities, or using other social media platforms for product comparison.

v. Operating in any other way for the purpose of transmitting leads to entities involved in the insurance business, except as specified in the regulations.

1.12.8 Rules for Insurance Web Aggregators

i. Every Insurance Web Aggregator must include the term 'Insurance Web Aggregator' or 'Insurance Web Aggregators' in its name to show its activity and help people tell the difference between IRDA licensed insurance Web Aggregators and other non-licensed entities related to insurance. When new companies apply to be insurance Web Aggregators, they must follow this naming rule.

ii. All approved insurance Web Aggregators must show their registered name, address, and the IRDA license number and its expiration date in all their communications with others.

iii. Insurance Web Aggregators are not allowed to use any other names in their communications or materials without getting the Authority's permission first.

1.12.9 Rules for Insurers and Web Aggregators

Insurers who want to get leads from web aggregators must sign an "agreement" with a web aggregator approved by the Authority. This agreement must cover details about:

i. How leads will be shared
ii. The responsibilities of both parties in following laws and regulations
iii. What information will be shared, like the name of the potential customer or client and their contact details
iv. When the insurer will provide information about the products agreed upon
v. The agreement will last for three years from the date it starts, as long as the web aggregator's license is valid.
vi. The web aggregator must report the agreement to the Authority within 15 days after signing it.

1.13 Role of Regulators

1.13.1 Insurance Regulatory and Development Authority of India

The Insurance Regulatory and Development Authority of India (IRDAI) is a self-governing, statutory organization responsible for overseeing and advancing the insurance and reinsurance sectors in India. It was established by the Insurance Regulatory and Development Authority of India Act, 1999, a law passed by the Indian government. The agency's main office is in Hyderabad, Telangana, which it moved to from Delhi in 2001.

IRDAI is made up of a 10-member board, including the chairman, five full-time members, and four part-time members, all appointed by the Indian government.

In ancient India, the concept of insurance was discussed in the works of Manu (Manusmrithi), Yagnavalkya (Dharmasastra), and Kautilya (Arthashastra), which explored the idea of pooling resources for redistribution following events like fires, floods, epidemics, and famines. The life-insurance sector got its start in 1818 with the creation of the Oriental Life Insurance Company in Calcutta, which unfortunately failed by 1834. Around the same time, in 1829, Madras Equitable began offering life-insurance services in the Madras Presidency. The British

Insurance Act of 1870 led to the establishment of Bombay Mutual (1871), Oriental (1874), and Empire of India (1897) in the Bombay Presidency. This period was primarily dominated by British-owned companies.

In 1914, the Indian government started publishing the financial reports of insurance companies. The Indian Life Assurance Companies Act of 1912 was the initial law to regulate life insurance. By 1928, the Indian Insurance Companies Act was passed to allow the government to gather statistical data on life and non-life insurance activities in India by both Indian and foreign insurers, including provident insurance societies. In 1938, the Insurance Act was consolidated and updated with detailed regulations to oversee insurer activities.

In 1950, the Indian government initiated the process of publishing the financial statements of insurance companies. The Insurance Amendment Act of 1950 led to the abolition of principal agencies, yet competition remained high, with claims of unfair business practices. The government then decided to nationalize the insurance sector.

On January 19, 1956, an ordinance was issued to nationalize the life-insurance sector, leading to the creation of the Life Insurance Corporation. This entity absorbed 154 Indian and 16 foreign insurers along with 75 provident societies, establishing a monopoly until the late 1990s when the insurance sector was opened up to private players.

The history of general insurance in India can be traced back to the Industrial Revolution in the West and the expansion of maritime trade in the 17th century. It was introduced as a legacy of British rule, with its origins dating back to the 1850 founding of the Triton Insurance Company in Calcutta. In 1907, the Indian Mercantile Insurance was established, becoming the first company to cover all types of general insurance. In 1957, a division of the Insurance Association of India was formed, setting a code of ethics and business standards.

Eleven years later, the Insurance Act was revised to oversee investments and set minimum solvency requirements, and the Tariff Advisory Committee was established. In 1972, with the enactment of the General Insurance Business (Nationalisation) Act, the insurance industry was nationalized on January 1, 1973. A hundred seven insurers were merged and organized into four entities: National Insurance Company, New India Assurance Company, Oriental Insurance Company, and United India Insurance Company. The General Insurance Corporation of India was established in 1971, with its operations commencing on January 1, 1973.

The insurance industry began to reopen in the early 1990s. In 1993, the government established a committee led by the former governor of the Reserve Bank of India, R. N. Malhotra, to suggest ways to improve insurance policies, in addition to the reforms started in the financial sector. This committee's report was submitted in 1994, recommending that the insurance sector allow private companies to join. It suggested that foreign companies could enter by creating Indian companies, preferably in partnerships with Indian entities.

Following the Malhotra Committee's suggestions, in 1999, the Insurance Regulatory and Development Authority (IRDA) was formed to oversee and develop the insurance sector, and it was officially established in April 2000. The IRDA's goals include fostering competition to increase customer satisfaction through more choices and lower prices, while also ensuring the financial stability of the insurance market.

After the Malhotra Committee's proposals, in August 2000, the IRDA opened the market to registration applications, permitting foreign companies to own up to 26 percent. The authority, with the authority to create rules under Section 11 of the Insurance Act, 1938, has since created regulations covering everything from company registrations to the protection of policyholders' interests since then.

In December 2000, the subsidiaries of the General Insurance Corporation of India were reorganized into independent entities, and the GIC transformed into a national reinsurer. By July 2002, Parliament approved a bill that separated the four subsidiaries of the GIC from the corporation. Currently, there are 28 general insurance companies and 24 life insurance companies operating in India, including the Export Credit Guarantee Corporation of India and the Agriculture Insurance Corporation of India. The insurance sector contributes about seven percent to India's GDP through its banking services.

In 2013, the IRDAI aimed to increase the foreign direct investment (FDI) limit in the insurance sector to 49 percent from its present 26 percent. The FDI limit in the insurance sector was increased to 100 percent as part of the budget 2019.

1.13.2 Goals of IRDA

- To advocate for the interests and rights of policyholders.
    - To foster and ensure the expansion of the Insurance Industry.
    - To guarantee the prompt resolution of legitimate claims and to prevent fraudulent activities and unethical practices.
    - To introduce transparency and maintain orderly operations in financial markets related to insurance.

1.13.3 Roles and Responsibilities of IRDA

The responsibilities of the IRDAI are outlined in Section 14 of the IRDAI Act, 1999, and encompass:
    - Issuing, renewing, altering, revoking, suspending, or cancelling registrations.
    - Safeguarding the interests of policyholders.
    - Establishing qualifications, codes of conduct, and training requirements for intermediaries and agents.
    - Setting standards for the conduct of surveyors and loss assessors.
    - Promoting operational efficiency in insurance businesses.
    - Regulating professional organizations associated with the insurance and reinsurance sectors.
    - Collecting fees and other charges.
    - Conducting inspections and investigations of insurers, intermediaries, and related entities.
    - Setting rates, benefits, conditions, and terms for insurers not under the jurisdiction of the Tariff Advisory Committee under section 641.1 of the Insurance Act, 1938 (4 of 1938).
    - Specifying record-keeping requirements.
    - Regulating the investment of insurer funds.
    - Regulating a margin of solvency.
    - Resolving disputes between insurers and intermediaries or insurance intermediaries.
    - Overseeing the Tariff Advisory Committee.
    - Determining the percentage of premium income allocated to support and regulate professional organizations.
    - Determining the proportion of life and general insurance business conducted in rural or social sectors.
    - Determining the format and method for maintaining books of accounts and issuing statements of accounts by insurers and other insurer intermediaries.
    - Regulating the investment of insurer funds.
    - Regulating a margin of solvency.
    - Resolving disputes between insurers and intermediaries or insurance intermediaries.
    - Overseeing the Tariff Advisory Committee.
    - Determining the percentage of premium income allocated to support and regulate professional organizations.
    - Determining the proportion of life and general insurance business conducted in rural or social sectors.
    - Determining the format and method for maintaining books of accounts and issuing statements of accounts by insurers and other insurer intermediaries.

1.14 Key and distinct terms in the realms of life and non-life insurance

1.14.1 Life Insurance Key Terms

a. Policyholder: The policyholder is the individual who initiates the purchase of the life insurance policy and is responsible for the premium payments.

The policyholder holds ownership of the policy and may or may not be the insured person. For example, a husband purchases a life insurance policy for his wife. Since the wife is the one who stays at home and takes care of the household, the husband is the one who makes the premium payments, making him the policyholder, and the wife is the insured.

b. Sum Assured (Coverage): Life insurance is designed to offer a death benefit to the insured.

The financial compensation that the insurer agrees to provide in the event of the insured person's death or any other specified insured events is known as 'Sum Assured'.

c. Policy Term: The 'policy term' refers to the length of time the policy is in effect for providing life insurance protection. The policy term can vary from one year to a lifetime, depending on the type of life insurance policy and its specific terms and conditions. Often, it is also called the policy duration or term.

The policy term determines the duration for which the insurance company will cover the risk. However, for whole life insurance policies, the coverage continues as long as the insured person is alive.

d. Nominee: The nominee is the designated individual (legal heir) chosen by the policyholder to receive the sum assured and other benefits from the life insurance company in the event of the insured person's death. The nominee can be a spouse, child, parent, etc. of the policyholder. The nominee is required to file a claim for the life insurance benefits if the insured person passes away during the policy term.

e. Premium: The premium is the fee paid by the policyholder to maintain the life insurance policy and ensure ongoing coverage. Failure to pay the premium on time, including during the grace period, can result in the policy being terminated.

There are various methods for paying the premium, including regular payments, limited payment terms, and single payments.

f. Maturity Age: The maturity age refers to the age at which a life insurance policy comes to an end or is terminated. It's akin to the policy's term length, but it describes the duration the policy remains active. Essentially, the insurance company specifies the highest age at which it will continue to provide life insurance to the insured. For example, if you're 30 years old and choose a term policy with a maturity age of 65, your policy will cover you until you reach 65. This means that for someone 30, the longest possible term length is 35 years.

1.14.2 Terms and Conditions of Automobile Insurance

The rules for auto insurance differ from one state to another, but understanding these key terms can be beneficial when looking for car insurance:

a. Insured: This term refers to the individuals or entities protected by the insurance policy.

b. Premiums: These are the regular monthly or yearly payments required to maintain the insurance coverage.

c. Deductible: This is the amount you have to pay upfront for any damages, like those from a crash, before your insurance coverage begins to cover the costs. Collision Coverage: This is the coverage that covers the repair costs of your car if it's damaged in a crash with another vehicle or object.

d. Comprehensive Coverage: This coverage is for damages to your car from fire, theft, vandalism, or other specified incidents.

e. Medical Payments Coverage: This coverage helps pay for the medical bills and funeral expenses for anyone covered by your policy who is injured in an accident, no matter who is at fault.

f. Uninsured Motorist Coverage: This coverage helps with the costs of injuries, including death, for you and others in your vehicle if you're hit by a driver without insurance who is at fault.

g. Bodily Injury Coverage: This coverage helps with the medical bills and funeral costs of others injured or killed in an accident for which you are responsible.

1.14.3 Understanding Health Insurance Terms

The Patient Protection and Affordable Care Act has made it easier for more Americans to access health insurance that is both high-quality and affordable. The government-run marketplaces are a key location for individuals to compare different insurance plans. Here are some essential terms related to health insurance:

a. Insured: The individual(s) protected by the insurance policy.

b. Deductible: The yearly sum you have to pay out of pocket for medical costs before your insurance begins to cover the expenses.

c. Premiums: The regular monthly or yearly payments required to maintain your insurance coverage.

d. Co-payment: A set fee you have to pay for each doctor's visit, with your insurance company covering the rest of the bill. For instance, you might have to pay a co-payment for each doctor's appointment.

e. Coinsurance: The percentage of the medical bill you are responsible for after you've satisfied your yearly deductible.

1.15 Understanding Insurance Customers

1.15.1 Insurance Customers and their Buying Patterns

People have access to a multitude of tools that may assist them from the point of discovery to the moment of purchase when it comes time to acquire or renew insurance. These days, conventional phone calls and in-person interactions with insurance brokers can be substituted by internet methods.

Compared to more deliberate expenditures like vacations or consumer products like makeup, the combined road to buying home and auto insurance is more complicated. It can also occur in a relatively short amount of time and is frequently linked to other significant purchases, such a house or automobile. Insurance companies must thus always be in the forefront of consumers' minds when they need to make a purchase.

We set out to learn more about the attitudes and goals of consumers and potential customers at each stage of the insurance purchasing process—discovery, assessment, comparison, and purchase—in order to assist marketers in better understanding how their target audience navigates this road. Facebook IQ commissioned Accenture to conduct a study of 996 insurance consumers in India who purchased property or auto insurance products in the three months before July 2018, with a focus on the impact that internet and mobile platforms play throughout the purchasing cycle.

How do people discover insurance brands and products?

In addition to doing so out of need, people frequently acquire insurance products in conjunction with the acquisition or renting of a home or vehicle. The discovery phase may thus likewise be brief. According to the report, 62% of consumers only initially evaluate one to three insurance brands, and 77% of consumers claim they are devoted to a certain insurance brand. In fact, compared to repeat customers who evaluate a smaller range of brands, first-time insurance buyers are 1.5 times more likely to explore five brands or more. This implies a chance to establish a connection with consumers who are not yet brand loyal, especially for new insurance products and brands.

For first-time purchasers, the internet is the most popular source of discovery; on their computer, tablet, or smartphone, 61% of consumers purchasing auto insurance and 76% of customers purchasing property insurance discover new brands and products. Furthermore, 47% of insurance consumers find and assess insurance businesses through talks with friends and family, demonstrating how much they rely on the collective knowledge.

These discussions with friends and family frequently take place online, and social media sites are crucial in helping them learn about new insurance companies and policies. The survey revealed that 77% of people discover property insurance brands and products on the Facebook family of apps2 and that 69% of them say they are more likely to be interested in an insurance brand or product they see advertised on Facebook and other social platforms.

What factors do consumers consider when assessing insurance companies and their offerings?

While insurance brokers continue to be a key resource for individuals seeking insurance coverage, three digital platforms stand out as crucial during the decision-making process. The findings indicate that 56% of individuals purchasing property insurance mention their mobile devices as a significant tool in assessing both the quality and reputation of insurance companies and their products. Specifically, for car insurance, first-time buyers are 1.4 times more inclined than those with previous purchases to view their mobile devices as a key tool in the evaluation process.

What aspects matter most to consumers when selecting insurance?

Investors consider various elements to be important when researching and evaluating insurance brands and products:

1.15.2 Digital capabilities:

This indicates broader trends in the industry and signals the necessity for all insurance providers to adjust to evolving expectations. The digital presence of an insurer plays a crucial role, especially for new customers. However, this digital presence extends beyond the purchase phase, with brands also needing to focus on the customer experience after buying. Many customers prefer to avoid the hassle of filling out a 20-page claims form after purchasing insurance online.

1.15.3 Personalization and on-demand insurance:

The option to create an insurance plan that suits their specific needs, rather than being locked into a one-size-fits-all policy, is particularly attractive to younger demographics.

Price, service quality, and company reputation:

Our research revealed that these elements continue to be significant considerations for all consumers. Surprisingly, while 85% of individuals prioritize price when choosing an insurer or insurance package, only 41% of insurance agents offer an online quote service.

How do consumers purchase insurance?

Our survey found that the majority of insurance purchases occur online: 44% of those buying car insurance and 49% of those purchasing property insurance do so through digital platforms. Given the importance of online channels in the buying process, insurance companies must adapt and ensure their purchasing experience is straightforward and smooth.

What does this mean for marketers?

Focus on creating mobile-friendly, seamless online experiences.

More than half of the respondents mentioned that a user-friendly application process is a key factor in their insurance buying decision. Streamline the application process and integrate digital solutions across all customer touchpoints to reduce wait times and address other pain points for a seamless journey.

Explore instant communication options.

Use new technologies to make sure agents are readily available to offer personalized advice and recommendations at every step of the process.

Anticipate the unique needs of your target audience.

To capture the attention of millennial buyers, use platforms where they are actively seeking insurance products. Make your brand stand out by emphasizing personalized packages and unique product features to steer customers away from price-only decisions and provide more engaging, relevant experiences through personalized messaging.

1.15.4 Determining Divisions within Insurance Clients

Insurance Promotion

The promotion of insurance services with a focus on enhancing customer focus and profit generation is known as Insurance Promotion. The primary emphasis in Insurance Promotion is on creating the perfect blend for the insurance sector. This involves improving both core and supplementary services through an appropriate service mix. The marketing approach allows insurance companies to grow their business while benefiting society and the company itself.

Lowering prices to compete does not necessarily mean better value for the consumer. Interactions with customers have become brief and transaction-oriented, while the focus on long-term value creation and engagement has decreased.

From the insurer's viewpoint, there's a different issue at play. The decision-making process within the typical organizational framework of many insurers is not well-suited to offer competitive premiums and manage both volume and a healthy combined ratio.

This issue arises from conflicting interests among departments, particularly the marketing and actuarial departments. The marketing team is primarily concerned with increasing volume. Their goal is to attract as many new customers as possible and expand the insurer's portfolio. On the other hand, the actuarial team aims to maintain a healthy portfolio where claim expenses do not exceed premium income. These divergent goals have led the insurer into a cycle of challenges. The marketing team targets a broad market with the premiums received from the actuarial team, failing to consider the differences in risk profiles and, as a result, attracting customers with high-risk profiles that threaten the combined ratio. In response, the actuarial team is forced to raise premiums generally, which, in turn, makes it more difficult for the marketing team to attract profitable customers, as these profiles are more likely to receive better offers from competitors who consider risk profiles and can offer lower premiums for low-risk profiles. This cycle, driven by different departmental incentives, is detrimental to the organization as a whole.

Breaking Down the Silos

To regain profitability and also increase the size of their portfolios, insurers must begin to think beyond the current silos and make business decisions that optimize the organization as a whole. Decisions should be made from a customer perspective, taking into account all available information within the organization, rather than being made in isolation. By adopting this approach, insurers can truly become customer-focused and end the cycle of challenges.

Dividing the Insurance Market

How can the actuarial and marketing teams work together to draw in the right clients? Which clients are adding to the profitability of the portfolio and are open to long-term partnerships? By analyzing the data available within the company, profitable groups of customers can be identified by dividing the portfolio based on expected Customer Lifetime Value. Data Science and Machine Learning methods can be applied to find new customers in the market who are valuable over their lifetime, drawing insights from the current portfolio. Algorithms that analyze the existing portfolio can identify customer characteristics that are high or low risk. Armed with this information, the marketing department can target similar customers with low-risk profiles, thereby enhancing the combined ratio. This, in turn, allows for lower premiums, boosting the company's competitive advantage. Additionally, marketing strategies can be customized for specific segments to ensure a better match between the insurance product and the policyholder, increasing the value for the policyholder and fostering loyalty.

Dividing the Insurance Market

The insurance market is segmented into various customer groups, with each product or service customized to meet the specific needs of each group. This segmentation enables the insurance company to divide the market into smaller segments where customer needs are uniform.

The insurance market is further divided into segments and sub-segments, including:

- Household sector
- Industrial sector
- Trade sector
- Institutional sector
- Region-wise sector
- Rural sector

Within the household sector, it is further divided into:

- Salaried class
- Self-employed
- Retired employees

Similarly, the industrial sector is divided into:

- Public sector
- Private sector

The other segments are also broken down into appropriate sub-segments.

1.15.5. *The importance of dividing the market for insurance companies*

a. Dividing the market is crucial for insurance companies. In the insurance industry, the main focus is on the policyholders. The goal of insurance marketing is to convert potential customers into policyholders. Dividing the market allows insurance marketers to understand the expectations of policyholders better.

b. Insurance companies take advantage of market opportunities to grow their market presence. Dividing the market in the insurance sector helps in identifying, understanding, and convincing different groups of potential customers.

c. Insurance professionals can operate in various market segments, including rural and urban areas, men and women, agricultural or industrial sectors, among others. Dividing the market makes it feasible to expand insurance services to the agricultural sector, which is mainly rural.

d. Dividing the market makes insurance companies aware of the evolving needs and demands of the rural sector, allowing them to tailor their services accordingly.

e. Understanding the market is key for insurance professionals, as the segmentation process aids in identifying the changing needs and demands of the rural sector.

f. Analyzing market segments helps insurance professionals develop effective marketing strategies. The product offerings can be customized to be more competitive, attracting more customers. Prospects will find the services more appealing.

g. Market segmentation enables insurance professionals to make their promotional efforts more creative and effective. It plays a key role in engaging prospects. Advertisers can create ads, messages, and campaigns that resonate with the target audience.

h. Dividing the market can also lead to more rational pricing decisions, benefiting the less privileged sections of society. Considering the points above, it's clear that market segmentation is essential for insurance professionals. It helps in converting prospects into policyholders.

1.16 Understanding How Customers Make Insurance Decisions

Key Moments

A widespread misunderstanding is that major life events are singular moments, when in reality, they are more like ongoing journeys for consumers: for instance, getting married might start with the idea of proposing and could extend to planning for future financial commitments, including family planning, with the wedding itself marking a significant step in this journey. Similarly, the process of buying a home can begin with the decision to purchase and may conclude with selling the property.

The Choice to Purchase

The decision to purchase insurance is influenced by more than just major life events and the quality of advice received. Those who choose not to buy insurance often cite reasons such as unclear benefits, complexity, and a lengthy application process. There's a noticeable gap between what potential buyers think about their immediate financial needs and the long-term financial advantages that come with having insurance.

Customer Loyalty Matters

Customer loyalty is crucial for business success. Companies that earn the trust of their customers tend to retain them longer, purchase more products, and recommend the company to others. Higher levels of loyalty lead to lower customer turnover, which can help companies cut costs and increase profits.

In recent years, insurers have focused on building customer loyalty. They've adopted digital platforms, trained their staff, and redesigned the customer experience. These efforts can be rewarding. Our research indicates that insurers who prioritize building loyalty can see their Net Promoter Scores increase by up to 20 percentage points over three years. On the other hand, those who neglect this focus may see their loyalty scores decline by similar amounts.

Insurers need to adjust their service hours to better serve customers, especially those using digital channels, as users are always online, and quick responses can be crucial.

Some companies have introduced chatbots as a first point of contact, while others have dedicated teams to assist online customers with any questions. The decision to invest in a dedicated team to support online customers 24/7 depends on the volume of interactions and transactions each company experiences.

The behaviour of customers at the pre-purchase stage significantly impacts insurance companies. Looking ahead, insurers must consider offering products and services tailored for online consumers, which could include features like KYC, automated underwriting, modular products for easy customization, digital identity verification, and more.

1.17 How Customers React When Making an Insurance Claim

When an insurance claim is filed, the way customers react can differ based on a number of factors:

a. **Immediate Reporting:** Some individuals quickly notify their insurance provider about the claim, while others might put it off due to reasons like not understanding the process or simply delaying.

b. **Reliability of Information:** The information provided by customers can be either complete or lacking. Accurate information speeds up the claim process, whereas incomplete or incorrect details can cause delays or even lead to the claim being denied.

c. **Emotional Response:** The emotional reaction of customers can range from distress to relief, depending on the claim's nature and severity.

d. **Expectations:** The expectations of customers regarding the claim process, such as how long it will take, what documents are needed, and how much they will receive, can affect their behavior. If these expectations are not met, it can lead to dissatisfaction and negative feedback.

e. **Preferred Communication Methods:** Customers might prefer to communicate through phone, email, or mobile applications. Insurance companies must adjust their communication methods to meet these varied preferences.

f. **Follow-Up and Feedback:** Some customers actively check on the progress of their claims and share their experiences with the claims process. Positive experiences can foster loyalty and referrals, while negative experiences can harm the insurer's reputation.

g. **Attempted Fraud:** Occasionally, customers might try to commit insurance fraud by exaggerating their losses or providing false information. Insurance companies use various strategies, including claims investigation and fraud detection algorithms, to prevent such actions.

h. **Behaviour After Claim Resolution:** Following the settlement of a claim, customers may reevaluate their insurance coverage, modify their approach to risk management, or even switch insurers based on their satisfaction with the claims process.

1.18 The Significance of Ethical Conduct in the Insurance Industry

The Insurance Institute promotes the highest ethical and professional standards across the insurance and financial services sector globally.

The governing body and its members expect all members to adhere to these standards and to preserve the Institute's reputation by adhering to this Code of Ethics and Conduct (the Code), which outlines the principles that members must follow in their professional roles.

Members are required to follow this Code. Failure to do so could lead to the Institute taking disciplinary measures against the member. The core values that define the expectations for members' behaviour towards key stakeholders in sections 1 to 5 include:

a. Acting responsibly and with integrity in their professional lives, considering their broader responsibilities to society. Interacting with others in a respectful, honest, and fair manner. Being reliable and ensuring their actions do not prioritize their own interests or those of others over the legitimate needs of their stakeholders;

b. Adhering to all relevant laws (including those of the Institute) and fulfilling the obligations of all relevant regulatory bodies, as well as adhering to appropriate codes of practice and conduct.

c. Demonstrating professional expertise and care, which includes: Achieving the technical and professional standards related to their qualifications, roles, and responsibilities; Performing their duties with the necessary skill, care, and diligence;

d. Maintaining professional standards in all interactions and relationships;

e. Respecting the confidentiality of information;

f. Maintaining objectivity in professional decisions and in providing opinions and statements, ensuring that personal bias or the influence of others does not compromise objectivity.

Members are also expected to respect the traditions and cultures of the countries in which they operate. They should conduct business in each country according to all relevant local laws, rules, and regulations. In situations where local customs conflict with the values stated above, the Code will serve as a guide to assist members in acting professionally.

A member in a professional capacity has responsibilities, stemming from these key values, towards various groups. In these relationships, a member should always act ethically, and their behaviour and conduct should align with the following principles:

Relations with clients

Members are committed to building and preserving trust with their clients at all times and should:

- Give each customer their due consideration and prioritize their needs fairly;
- Gather and share all relevant information, respecting their privacy;
- Resolve any conflicts of interest between personal gains or those of affiliated entities, ensuring the best interests of all clients;
- Exercise caution, skill, and thoroughness in all actions;
- Stick to their areas of expertise and any given permissions;
- Maintain financial integrity and safeguard any funds or assets on behalf of clients;
- Be transparent, respectful, and attentive to all clients, offering them the respect and attention they deserve;
- Be truthful and reliable in all communications with clients;
- Offer unbiased and helpful advice to clients;
- Follow all legal and regulatory standards in providing goods and services to clients;
- Avoid accepting or giving any form of payment, gifts, entertainment, loans, or preferential treatment to clients or potential clients, except for occasional gifts, entertainment, or compensation, which are part of standard business practices and do not interfere with their obligations to clients.

Interactions at the workplace

Members are dedicated to fostering positive relationships with their employers and colleagues and should:

- Prevent any conflicts of interest between personal interests and the obligations to their employer;
- Use any information obtained as an employee responsibly and protect their employer's confidential information;
- Act with integrity and reliability in their professional duties;
- Be open, fair, and respectful towards all colleagues, employees, customers, and suppliers, treating everyone equally and providing them with the same respect and opportunities;
- Seek continuous improvement in their professional skills and knowledge;
- Provide complete and accurate records of all business transactions with their employer;
- Avoid receiving or giving any form of payment, gifts, entertainment, loans, or preferential treatment to suppliers or business associates, except for occasional gifts, entertainment, or compensation, which are part of standard business practices and do not compromise their duties to their employer.

Moreover, when a member occupies a role of authority within a company, they ought to:

- Facilitate, or motivate their employer to establish appropriate mechanisms for the internal examination of decisions, policies, and actions whenever an employee brings up ethical issues. (Employees should not face consequences for speaking up about ethical concerns, even if this leads to a disadvantage for the company or a customer);
- Include, or motivate their employer to include, ethical principles in the company's rules for governance, which should also encompass the creation of a code of ethics.

- Refrain from sharing any information from their employer or the organization that is confidential or sensitive in written tasks.

IMPORTANT QUESTIONS

Short Answer Questions (3-4 marks each):

1. Define risk and differentiate between actual and consequential losses.
2. Explain two methods of managing risk.
3. Briefly describe the risks of dying early and living too long.
4. List four different classes of insurance.
5. Why is insurance considered important?
6. How do individuals and insurers manage risks differently?
7. What factors are considered while fixing insurance premiums?
8. What is reinsurance and why is it used?
9. Explain the role of insurance in promoting economic development and social security.
10. Name three constituents of the insurance market.

Long Answer Questions (8-10 marks each):

1. Explain the concept of risk management and its various stages.
2. Discuss the importance of ethical behaviour in the insurance industry.
3. Describe the operations of insurance companies and intermediaries.
4. Analyze the role of regulators in the insurance market.
5. Differentiate between common terms used in life and non-life insurance with suitable examples.
6. Explain how understanding customer behaviour at the purchase point and during claims can benefit insurers.

OBJECTIVE TYPE QUESTIONS

Multiple Choice Questions (MCQs):

1. Which of the following is NOT a type of risk?

   a) Financial Risk
b) Strategic Risk
c) Opportunity Risk
d) Legal Risk
   2. Actual loss refers to:
   a) The fear of a negative event
b) The financial cost of a negative event

c) The emotional impact of a negative event

d) All of the above

3. Risk management involves:

   a) Identifying risks

b) Assessing risks

c) Developing strategies to mitigate risks

d) All of the above

4. What type of insurance protects against the financial burden of living a longer life than expected?

   a) Term Life Insurance

b) Long-Term Care Insurance

c) Annuities

d) Whole Life Insurance

5. The premium for an insurance policy is determined by factors like:

   a) Age and health

b) Type of coverage

c) Risk profile

d) All of the above

6. Reinsurance is a practice where:

   a) An insurance company shares risk with another company

b) An individual reduces their risk by purchasing insurance

c) The government provides financial security

d) A company transfers all its risk to another company

7. How does insurance contribute to economic development?

   a) By providing capital for investment

b) By reducing uncertainty for businesses

c) By promoting financial stability

d) All of the above

8. Intermediaries in the insurance market include:

   a) Agents

b) Brokers

c) Both A and B

d) Regulators

9. An example of a specialist insurance company is:

a) Life insurer
b) Health insurer
c) Both A and B
d) Property and Casualty insurer

10. Ethical behaviour in insurance involves:

    a) Acting in the best interest of the customer
    b) Disclosing all relevant information
    c) Avoiding fraud and misrepresentation
    d) All of the above

11. The insurance market consists of:

    a) Insurers only
    b) Insureds only
    c) Insurers, intermediaries, and regulators
    d) Reinsurance companies only

12. Insurance companies typically generate income through:

    a) Premiums collected
    b) Investment returns
    c) Both A and B
    d) Neither A nor B

13. Insurance intermediaries like agents and brokers help:

    a) Sell insurance policies
    b) Advise clients on coverage
    c) Process claims
    d) All of the above

14. Specialist insurance companies focus on covering:

    a) Specific niche risks
    b) A broad range of risks
    c) Life insurance only
    d) Property insurance only

15. Regulators play a crucial role in:

    a) Setting industry standards
    b) Protecting consumers
    c) Ensuring solvency of insurers
    d) All of the above

Fill in the Blanks (20 marks)

1. The process of identifying, analysing, and controlling risks is called ______________. (Risk management)
2. An unexpected event that may cause financial loss is called a(n) ______________. (Risk)
3. The actual financial cost incurred due to a negative event is called a(n) ______________ loss. (Actual)
4. The additional financial losses resulting from an insured event are called ______________ losses. (Consequential)
5. Individuals can manage risks by ______________, ______________, and ______________. (avoiding risky activities, saving money, having an emergency fund)
6. When an insurance company pays you for a covered loss, it is called ______________. (Indemnity)
7. The amount paid by the policyholder to the insurance company for coverage is called a(n) ______________. (Premium)
8. Reinsurance allows an insurance company to share a large risk with another company called a ______________ company. (Reinsurance)
9. The government agency that supervises the insurance industry is called the ______________. (Regulator)
10. People who sell insurance policies and work for a specific insurance company are called ______________. (Agents)
11. An agreement to financially protect someone from a potential loss in exchange for a regular payment is called ______________.
12. The unexpected event that may cause a loss is referred to as a(n) ______________.
13. When a risk actually happens and results in a financial loss, it's called an ______________ loss.
14. The process of identifying, analysing, and taking steps to address risks is called ______________ management.
15. ______________ insurance provides financial protection in case of death.

ANSWERS

Multiple Choice Questions

1. (d) Legal Risk
2. (b) The financial cost of a negative event
3. (d) All of the above
4. (b) Long-Term Care Insurance
5. (d) All of the above
6. (a) An insurance company shares risk with another company
7. (d) All of the above
8. (c) Both A and B
9. (d) Property and Casualty insurer
10. (d) All of the above
11. (c) Insurers, intermediaries, and regulators
12. (c) Both A and B
13. (d) All of the above
14. (a) Specific niche risks
15. (d) All of the above

Fill in the Blanks

1. Risk management
2. Risk
3. Actual
4. Consequential
5. Avoiding risky activities, saving money, having an emergency fund
6. Indemnity
7. Premium
8. Reinsurance
9. Regulator
10. Agents
11. Insurance contract (or policy)
12. Peril (or insured event)
13. Actual
14. Risk
15. Life

CHAPTER TWO

INSURANCE CONTRACT AND INSURANCE PRODUCTS

2.1. Basic and specialized terms in both Life and Non-Life Insurance Policies

2.1.1. Life Insurance Terms

- **Policyholder:** The policyholder is the individual who initiates the purchase of the life insurance policy and is responsible for paying the premiums. The policyholder owns the policy and may or may not be the insured person. For example, a husband purchases a life insurance policy for his wife. Since the wife is the one who stays at home and takes care of the household, the husband is the one who makes the premium payments, making him the policyholder, and the wife is the insured person.
- **Policy Term:** The 'policy term' refers to the length of time the policy is in effect, providing life insurance coverage. This term can vary from one year to 100 years or even a lifetime, depending on the type of life insurance policy and its specific terms and conditions. It is also known as the policy duration or the policy period. The policy term determines the duration the insurance company will cover the risk. However, in the case of whole-life insurance policies, the coverage continues as long as the insured person is alive.
- **Beneficiary:** The beneficiary is the person (legal heir) named by the policyholder to receive the sum assured and other benefits in the event of the insured person's death. The beneficiary can be a spouse, child, parent, or any other individual specified by the policyholder. If the insured person passes away during the policy term, the beneficiary is entitled to claim the benefits.
- **Premium:** The premium is the fee paid by the policyholder to maintain the life insurance policy and ensure ongoing coverage. Failure to pay the premium on time, including during the grace period, can result in the policy being terminated. There are various payment methods for premiums, including regular payments, limited payment terms, and single payments.
- **Maturity Age:** This refers to the age at which a policy comes to an end or ceases. It's akin to the policy's duration but describes the length of time the policy remains active. Essentially, the insurance company specifies the highest age at which the insured will continue to receive benefits from the policy. For example, if you're 30 years old and choose a term policy with a maturity age of 65, your policy will cover you until you reach 65. This means your policy's longest duration for someone 30 years old is 35 years.

2.1.2. Terms and Definitions for Car Insurance

The rules for car insurance can differ from one state to another, but understanding these basic terms can be useful when looking for car insurance:

- **Insured:** This is the individual or individuals protected by the insurance policy.
- **Premiums:** These are the monthly or yearly payments required to maintain the insurance coverage.
- **Deductible:** This is the amount you have to pay out of pocket for any damages, like those from a crash, before your insurance starts covering the costs.
- **Collision Coverage:** This coverage pays for the repair of your car if it's damaged in a crash with another vehicle or object.
- **Comprehensive Coverage:** This coverage covers the cost of repairs for your car if it's damaged by fire, theft, vandalism, or other specified events.
- **Medical Payments Coverage:** This coverage covers the medical and funeral expenses for anyone covered by your policy who is injured in an accident, no matter who is at fault.
- **Uninsured Motorist Coverage:** This coverage pays for your injuries and/or the death of you and others in your vehicle if you're hit by a driver without insurance who is at fault.
- **Bodily Injury Coverage:** This coverage pays for the medical bills and/or funeral costs of others injured or killed in an accident for which you are responsible.

2.1.3. Understanding Health Insurance Terms

The Patient Protection and Affordable Care Act has made it easier for more Americans to access high-quality, affordable health insurance. The government-run marketplaces are a key location for individuals to compare insurance plans. Here are some essential health insurance terms to know:

- **Insured:** This refers to the individuals or people covered by the insurance policy.
- **Deductible:** This is the yearly amount you have to pay out of pocket for medical expenses before your insurance starts covering the costs.
- **Premiums:** These are the monthly or yearly payments required to maintain your insurance coverage.
- **Co-payment:** This is a fixed fee you pay for medical services, with your insurance company covering the rest of the bill. For instance, you might have to pay a co-payment for each doctor's visit.
- **Coinsurance:** This is the percentage of the medical bill you're responsible for after you've met your yearly deductible.

2.2. The Fundamentals of Insurance Contracts

The primary goal of insurance is mutual cooperation. Insurance is essentially the fair exchange of the risk of loss from one party to another in return for a premium.

 a. Nature of Contract: This principle is crucial in the formation of an insurance contract. It begins when one party offers or proposes a contract, and the other party agrees to it. For a contract to be valid, it must be straightforward. Willingly entering into by both parties is must.

 b. Principle of Utmost Good Faith: This principle requires both parties in an insurance contract to have trust in each other. As a policyholder, it's your responsibility to disclose all relevant information to your insurance company. Any deceit or false information can lead to the cancellation of the contract.

 c. Principle of Insurable Interest: This principle states that the person insured must have a direct interest in the subject matter of the insurance. If there's no insurable interest, the contract is considered void. An insurance company will not issue a policy if there's no insurable interest. This interest must be present at the time the insurance is purchased. For example, a creditor has an insurable interest in the life of a debtor, a person has an unlimited interest in their spouse's life, etc.

d. Principle of compensable loss: This principle underpins the concept of compensable loss, which refers to the provision of security or compensation for losses or damages. The rule in insurance holds that the insurance company should not reimburse an insured individual for more than their financial loss incurred. Thus, in insurance, the policyholder receives compensation equal to the actual financial loss, not the total loss. This rule serves as a regulatory foundation and is adhered to more rigorously in property insurance than in life insurance. The goal of this principle is to return the policyholder to their pre-loss financial state.

e. Principle of subrogation: The principle of subrogation allows the policyholder to seek payment from the party responsible for the loss from the insurer. It empowers the insurer to take legal action to recover the amount of the loss, for instance, if an individual sustains injuries in a car accident due to the negligence of another party, the insurance company is responsible for covering the costs and can then pursue legal action against the negligent party to recoup the funds expended on the claim.

f. Principle of double insurance: The principle of double insurance occurs when an individual is insured against the same peril by two distinct insurance companies or by the same insurer through separate policies. This scenario is permissible in insurance policies like fire, maritime, and property insurance that fall under indemnity contracts. The double insurance policy is utilized when the insurer's financial stability is uncertain. The insured is limited to receiving compensation for only the actual loss and cannot claim the full amount from both insurers.

g. Principle of proximate cause: Proximate cause, in a legal sense, means the 'closest cause' or 'direct cause.' This principle applies when the loss is caused by multiple factors. Proximate cause is defined as the leading cause that has the greatest impact on the loss, considering the series of causes contributing to the damage or loss. This principle is relevant when the damage or loss is a result of several events or circumstances.

2.3. Varieties of Life Insurance Products

a. Term Insurance Plan: Term insurance plans are purchased for a specific duration, such as 20 or 30 years. These policies lack cash value and do not provide maturity benefits, making them more affordable than other options. Their value only increases if the insured event occurs.

b. Endowment Policy: The primary distinction between a term insurance plan and an endowment policy is the additional benefit of receiving a lump sum if the insured person survives until the policy's maturity date. The details and features of a term policy also apply to an endowment policy.

c. Unit Linked Insurance Plan: These plans allow the policyholder to accumulate wealth alongside life insurance coverage. Premiums are divided into two parts: one for life insurance and another for wealth accumulation. The plan offers the option to partially withdraw the funds.

d. Money Back Policy: This policy is akin to an endowment policy, with the key difference being the inclusion of various survival benefits that are distributed over the policy term.

e. Whole Life Policy: Unlike other policies that have a set end date, a whole life policy lasts the insured's entire life. It also provides survival benefits to the insured. The policyholder can choose to partially withdraw the policy's value or borrow against it.

f. Annuity/ Pension Plan: With this plan, the premium paid is invested as assets, and the policyholder receives income in the form of annuity or a lump sum, as per their choice.

2.4. Understanding Life Insurance Concepts

Life insurance operates on several fundamental principles designed to balance the needs of the market, ensuring the profitability of insurance firms while providing coverage for policyholders.

In India, there are four primary principles of life insurance:

a. Insurable Interest: This principle focuses on the degree of interest a person has in a specific policy. This interest could be related to family ties, personal relationships, and more. Depending on the level of interest, an insurance company may decide to approve or deny an application to prevent policy misuse.

b. Law of Large Numbers: This principle is based on the theory that over time, large sample sizes lead to more stable outcomes and reduce the risk of losses.

c. Good Faith: Buying insurance is essentially entering into a contract between the insurer and the insured. It's crucial to conduct this transaction in good faith by providing all necessary information truthfully. Concealing any details from the insurer could lead to severe consequences for the insured in the future. Therefore, the insurer is obligated to explain every aspect of the policy, ensuring there are no hidden or undisclosed terms, and the insured is fully informed about all conditions.

d. Risk & Minimal Loss: Insurance is inherently risky, and companies must operate to make profits while considering the risk involved. The principle of minimal risk suggests that the insured individual should take steps to minimize their exposure to risks. This includes maintaining a healthy lifestyle, undergoing regular health check-ups, and more.

2.4.1. Key Factors to Consider for Life Insurance

a. Research: As a potential life insurance policyholder, you're presented with a wide range of policy options available. It's crucial to conduct thorough research before deciding on a policy to ensure you're getting the best deal and maximum benefits.

b. Review the Policy Details: The policy's terms and conditions outline all necessary information about the policy. It's important to carefully read and understand every detail before committing to a policy.

c. Be Aware of the Lock-In Period: Sometimes, people buy insurance policies without fully understanding them and later regret their decision. In such cases, some insurance companies offer a short return period, typically 15 days, during which you can return the policy and choose another if you're not satisfied.

d. Explore Payment Plans: Most insurance providers offer flexible payment plans, including annual, semi-annual, quarterly, or monthly. It's advisable to choose an Electronic Check System (ECS) payment method, which will automatically deduct the insurance premium from your bank account. Additionally, you can select a payment schedule that suits your convenience.

e. Be Completely Honest: It's important not to withhold any information when completing the insurance application form. Accurately disclose all personal details and medical history to the insurance company. Providing false information can lead to complications when filing claims in the future.

2.4.2. Leading Life Insurance Providers in India

Here are some of the leading life insurance companies in India:

a. LIC: Life Insurance Corporation of India
b. SBI Life Insurance
c. ICICI Prudential Life Insurance
d. HDFC Standard Life Insurance
e. Bajaj Allianz Life Insurance
f. Max Life Insurance
g. Birla Sun Life Insurance
h. Kotak Life Insurance

2.5. Understanding Life Insurance and Its Classification

In India, the average level of life insurance coverage and its concentration is quite low, standing at just 2.76%. While there have been some improvements in this area, the overall progress has been slow. A significant number of people are not fully aware of the advantages of life insurance, and the low coverage rates reflect this lack of awareness.

Accidents and unfortunate events highlight the vulnerability of human life and underscore the need for systematic protection through life insurance. It serves as a crucial asset for ensuring the financial security and well-being of a person's family. It acts as a shield to protect the dependents of the insured. Without life insurance, the family of the deceased faces the devastating loss of their loved one, along with various financial burdens such as mortgage payments, loan repayments, monthly instalments, and child support.

2.5.1. Key Elements of Life Insurance Plans

a. **Policyholder:** This is the individual who pays the monthly premiums for the life insurance policy and signs a contract with a life insurance company.
b. **Premium:** This is the amount the policyholder pays to the life insurance company for the protection of their life.
c. **Maturity:** This refers to the point in the policy term when the contract comes to an end.
d. **Insured:** This is the person whose life is insured. Upon their death, the insurance company is responsible for providing financial support to the dependents.
e. **Sum Assured:** This is the amount the insurance company will pay to the dependents of the insured if certain events, as outlined in the policy, occur.
f. **Policy Term:** This is the specific duration (mentioned in the policy) for which the insurance company offers life coverage, and it also indicates the active period of the contract.
g. **Nominee:** This is a person named in the policy who is entitled to receive the predetermined compensation as a part of the policy.
h. **Claim:** Should the insured pass away, the nominees can submit a claim to the insurance provider to receive the predetermined payout.

2.5.2. Categorization of Life Insurance Policies

a. Permanent Life Insurance Policies

Permanent life insurance is characterized by the policyholder paying premiums over their lifetime, with the promise that their beneficiaries will receive the policy's death benefit. This type of policy does not expire as long as the premiums are paid.

There are several variations of permanent life insurance policies:

- **Whole Life Insurance:** This policy requires the policyholder to make premium payments for their entire life, with the promise that their beneficiaries will receive the policy's death benefit.

- **Universal Life Insurance:** This policy offers flexibility in premium payments and death benefit amounts, allowing the policyholder to adjust these features as their financial situation changes.

- **Variable Life Insurance:** This policy allows the policyholder to invest the policy's cash value in various investment options, potentially increasing the policy's death benefit.

b. Term Life Insurance Policies

Term life insurance is designed for a specific period, typically ranging from 10 to 30 years. During this term, the policyholder pays premiums, and if they pass away, their beneficiaries receive the policy's death benefit.

There are several term life insurance policies:

- **Level Term Life Insurance:** This policy offers a fixed death benefit throughout the term, regardless of the policyholder's health or age.

- **Decreasing Term Life Insurance:** This policy's death benefit decreases over time, matching the policyholder's decreasing financial obligations.

- **Increasing Term Life Insurance:** This policy's death benefit increases over time, matching the policyholder's increasing financial obligations.

c. Endowment Life Insurance Policies

Endowment life insurance is a type of policy where the policyholder pays premiums for a set period, after which they receive the policy's death benefit. If the policyholder dies before the term end, then their nominees/beneficiaries receive the death benefit.

There are several variations of endowment life insurance policies:

- **Ordinary Endowment Life Insurance:** This policy has a fixed term, and the policyholder pays premiums until the term ends or until their death, whichever comes first. If the policyholder dies before the term ends, their beneficiaries receive the full death benefit.

- **Joint Endowment Life Insurance:** This policy involves two or more people, with the premiums being paid until the death of the last insured person.

- **Double Endowment Life Insurance:** This policy provides double the death benefit if the insured person dies before the term ends. If the insured person survives the term, they receive the full death benefit.

- **Pure Endowment Life Insurance:** This policy guarantees the policyholder will receive the death benefit after a specific term, regardless of their survival. If the policyholder dies before the term ends, their beneficiaries receive the full death benefit.

c. Term life insurance policy

- **Basic term life insurance policy:** This policy involves paying the premium in a single, lump sum payment. The coverage period is typically no more than two years; hence it's referred to as a temporary term life insurance policy. If the insured individual passes away before the policy's term ends, their beneficiary will receive the policy's death benefit. However, if the insured individual survives the policy term, they will not receive any payout.

- **Renewal term life insurance policy:** This policy allows for the renewal of coverage after the initial term has expired. The premium for this policy may be higher than the initial rate due to the increased age of the insured. There's no requirement for a new health or background check to renew the policy.

- **Convertible term life insurance policy:** This policy is designed for terms of 5, 6, or 7 years, similar to a term life insurance policy. It offers the option to convert the term life insurance policy into a whole life insurance policy or an endowment life insurance policy at any time.

d. Profit-sharing term life insurance policy

- In this policy, the insured individual receives the death benefit from the insurance company's profits, in addition to the policy's face value. This means that if the insured individual passes away before the policy's term ends, their beneficiary will receive both the policy's death benefit and the company's profits. However, if the insured individual survives the policy term, only the policy's death benefit will be paid out.

e. Term life insurance policies based on the number of insured individuals

- **Single life insurance policy:** This policy covers only one individual, treating the life of that person as the insured. It can be applied for in whole life insurance, endowment life insurance, and term life insurance.
- **Joint/ multiple life insurance policy:** This policy covers two or more individuals, such as spouses, partners in a business, or family members. It is also available in whole life insurance and endowment life insurance.

f. Based on the method of premium payment

- **Single premium life insurance:** In this policy, the insured individual pays the entire premium amount upfront to the insurance provider. There's no need to worry about making timely premium payments. This policy is often chosen by individuals who have unexpectedly won a large sum of money, such as through a lottery.
- **Routine premium life insurance:** With this policy, the insured individual makes regular premium payments to the insurance company until their death. Essentially, the insured person ensures that the premiums are paid on time to the insurance company.
- **Limited payment premium life insurance:** This policy allows the insured individual to make premium payments until their death, but the duration is shorter than the insured period.

g. Based on the amount of the insured sum

- **Single premium life insurance:** In this case, the insured individual receives the full amount of the policy at once. If all premiums have been paid, the beneficiary of the policy receives the full sum. However, if the total sum has not been paid, the beneficiary still receives the full amount.
- **Instalment payment policy:** This policy allows both the insured individual and their beneficiary to receive the policy's value in smaller, regular payments. It's particularly beneficial for older individuals who may not want to risk misusing a large lump sum.

2.5.3. Benefits of Life Insurance in India

a. Death Benefits: Life insurance provides a safety net for individuals and their families by covering the cost of the policy in the event of the insured's death. This coverage includes the policy's stated sum assured, along with any applicable bonuses, known as the death benefit.

b. **Investment Features:** Some whole life insurance policies offer the dual advantage of insurance and investment. Half of the premium goes towards insurance, while the other half is invested in stocks, bonds, or a mix of both. This feature allows policyholders to enjoy both protection and potentially high returns on their investments. By choosing funds that match their investment goals and risk tolerance, policyholders can optimize this aspect. Certain policies even allow for fund switching to adapt to changing objectives. The Invest 4G plan from Canara HSBC Oriental Bank of Commerce, for example, allows for selection from a variety of 7 unit-linked funds and different portfolio management options based on personal preference.

c. **Maturity Features:** Life insurance policies can also serve as a savings tool by providing maturity benefits. If the insured outlives the policy term without making any claims, the total premiums paid are returned at the policy's maturity. This feature allows the life insurance plan to act as a savings vehicle while also providing a protective benefit.

d. Tax Advantages: Life insurance policies fall under Section 80C of the Income Tax Act (ITA), which allows individuals to reduce their tax liabilities by investing in certain instruments, including term insurance. Premiums paid for a life insurance policy are eligible for a maximum tax deduction of up to Rs. 1.5 lakh under Section 80C. Additionally, any benefits received from the insurance policy are tax-free (subject to a premium not exceeding 10% of the Sum Assured, annually), as per Section 10(1 OD). For those with health-related riders, such as critical illness or surgical care riders, tax deductions are also available under Section 80Dofthe ITA.

e. Liability Coverage: To achieve personal and financial goals, individuals may need financial support in the form of loans, mortgages, and other debts. Whether it's student loans or credit card debt, managing these liabilities can be financially challenging without a stable income. While you might have the means to pay off a portion of your debts now, your family could struggle to handle these obligations in your absence due to the loss of income. Therefore, having a life insurance policy ensures that your family has the financial resources to continue making loan and mortgage payments, even after you're gone.

f. Riders: You have the option to add riders to boost the coverage of your life insurance policy. There are various riders available, from Critical Illness to Accidental Total Permanent Disability, which protect you and your family in situations where your life insurance might not be applicable. Today, life insurance and life insurance policies are essential. They serve as a tool for reducing risk and providing protection for both the insured and their dependents in various life situations. By understanding the main features and advantages of a life insurance policy, you can make a well-informed choice.

2.6 Annuities: Types of Annuities

The reason annuities come in so many different forms is because they are essentially agreements between the annuity owner, also known as the annuitant, and the insurance company. These agreements vary in terms of their provisions, costs, and payout structures. The benefit is that annuities can be tailored to meet your specific needs. However, the wide range of options can be daunting for those considering annuities. Annuities are agreements issued by financial institutions where the money is invested to provide a guaranteed income stream in the future. They are primarily used for retirement planning and help individuals manage the risk of running out of savings. After annuitization, the institution will start making payments to you at a later date. The three main types of annuities are fixed, variable, and fixed indexed. Understanding your risk tolerance can help you navigate the various annuity options available. The amount of risk you're willing to take affects the payment calculations. Lower risk leads to more predictable payments, while higher risk can result in potentially higher returns.

Type	Interest	Risk	Reward
Fixed	Preset/guaranteed	Low	Predictable
Variable	Tied to Investment portfolio	Higher	Potentially higher or lower
Fixed Indexed	Preset minimum. Can change according to index like stock market	Medium	Won't sink below the set level.

Types of Annuities

Constant Annuity

This choice offers the lowest level of risk and the highest degree of certainty. Constant annuities are equipped with a fixed, unchanging interest rate that remains constant throughout the agreement's duration. In contrast, other investments may experience significant increases or decreases in value. Nonetheless, the constant annuity maintains its stability. Occasionally, though, the interest rate may be adjusted after a specific period has elapsed.

2.6.1. Different Types of Fixed Annuities

An equity-indexed annuity is a specific kind of fixed annuity that resembles a mix of both. It guarantees a minimum interest rate, similar to a fixed annuity, but its value is also influenced by the performance of a chosen stock index, usually calculated as a percentage of that index's total return.

A market-value-adjusted annuity is designed to combine two key features: the option to select and lock in the duration and interest rate at which your annuity will grow, along with the ability to access funds from the annuity before it matures. This access to funds is made possible by adjusting the annuity's value to account for any changes in the interest rate "market" (i.e., the overall level of interest rates) from the annuity's start date to the date of withdrawal.

A variable annuity is associated with higher risks but also offers the potential for greater rewards. The interest rate of a variable annuity is linked to the performance of an investment portfolio. The amount of money received from a variable annuity can increase if the portfolio performs well, but it can also decrease if the investments suffer losses.

With a variable annuity, the insurance company invests in a variety of mutual funds selected by the policyholder. The success of these funds will determine the growth of the account and the eventual size of the payout to the policyholder. The payout from a variable annuity can either be fixed or change based on the account's performance.

Individuals who opt for variable annuities are prepared to take on some level of risk in the pursuit of higher returns. Typically, these annuities are recommended for those with a good understanding of different types of mutual funds and their associated risks.

2.6.2. Unique Features of Group Insurance/Superannuation Schemes

A superannuation scheme is designed to ensure that an employee continues to receive a steady income stream even after retirement. By contributing to a superannuation scheme, you can ensure that there is a pool of funds available to pay this benefit to your employees.

Many employers offer various retirement benefits to their employees, either due to legal requirements or as a voluntary measure to keep employees engaged for a longer duration. These retirement benefits can include provident fund gratuity, National Pension System, etc. Superannuation benefit is one such retirement benefit provided by employers to their employees.

- It helps in creating a dedicated fund for employees
- It protects the employer's working capital from large retirement pay-outs
- It offers tax advantages to both employees and employers

Often, employees overlook this retirement benefit, and some may not even be aware that they are entitled to a superannuation benefit since the contributions towards the benefit do not come out of their own pocket. Additionally, some may not be aware of the superannuation amount they will receive upon retirement. Given these circumstances, it's crucial to understand the superannuation benefit to facilitate better financial planning and retirement preparation.

2.6.3. Categories of Superannuation Benefits

In India, superannuation benefits are categorized based on their investment approach and the level of benefits they offer:

Defined Contribution Plans: These benefits differ from defined benefit plans. In a defined benefit plan, the benefit amount is set and known in advance, whereas a defined contribution plan has a set contribution amount, and the benefit amount is linked directly to the contribution and market conditions. These benefits are easier to manage, but the risk lies with the employee since they are uncertain about the retirement benefits, they will receive.

Defined Benefit Plans: The amount of benefit received is predetermined, regardless of the contributions made to the plan. The fixed benefit amount is determined by various factors, including the number of years worked at the company, salary, and the age at which the employee begins to receive benefits. These benefits are more complex and the risk of providing such benefits rests with the employer. Upon retirement, a qualified employee is entitled to a fixed sum, as determined by a pre-established formula, at regular intervals.

Exposure to Risks: A risk is a potential event or factor that could lead to a loss, such as the threat of a fire that might destroy a home. A hazard, on the other hand, is a factor or activity that could cause or increase the risk of loss, like leaving a can of gasoline near the house or failing to maintain the car's brakes.

Risk, peril, and hazard are terms used to describe the likelihood of a loss, and they are often used interchangeably, but the insurance sector differentiates between these terms. Risk simply refers to the possibility of a loss, while a peril is the cause of the loss. A hazard is a situation that heightens the risk of loss.

Peril implies danger and suggests an immediate threat. For instance, a rockslide poses a peril to anyone below the cliff as the rocks start to move.

In insurance policies, the specific risks covered are usually outlined. Commonly listed risks include fire, wind, water, and theft. However, it's important to note that the policy may exclude coverage for certain damages in specific situations, such as if the insured's negligence led to the damage or worsened it.

This often leads to disagreements between the insurance company and the insured. For example, the insurance company might refuse to cover roof damage after a storm, arguing that the insured did not replace the old roof.

This is often the root of disputes between the insurer and the insured. For example, the insurer might deny a claim for damage to the roof after a storm, claiming that the insured was negligent in not replacing the old roof.

Speculative risk stands out from straightforward risk because it carries the chance for both profit and loss, like when you invest in the stock market. The majority of speculative risks are not covered by insurance because people take them on with the hope of earning a profit. Additionally, speculative risks usually lead to more frequent losses compared to straightforward risks, as the only other potential outcome is profit. Therefore, while many individuals take steps to safeguard their well-being or their belongings, they still choose to take speculative risks, such as investing in the stock market, in pursuit of profit. This is because avoiding these activities that pose speculative risks could prevent most of them.

Legal risk is a specific kind of personal risk that involves the threat of legal action due to negligence, professional errors, or intentional harm to others or their property. Legal risk encompasses the financial consequences of being found responsible for damages or the costs associated with defending oneself, even if no financial liability is established. Most risks related to personal, property, and legal matters are covered by insurance.

Personal risks directly impact an individual, including health issues, disabilities, or death. Property risks pertain to damage or loss of personal or real estate. For example, a house fire or a car theft represent property risks, with property loss involving both direct damage to the property and the financial losses that follow. Direct damage is the actual harm to the property, while consequential losses are the financial repercussions of the direct damage. For instance, if your car is stolen, that's a direct damage; if you have to rent a car because of the theft, that's a consequential loss from renting a car.

Straightforward risk is one where the potential for loss is constant over a period, making it easier to predict and, thus, more suitable for insurance. These risks are known as static risks. In contrast, dynamic risks fluctuate over time, making them harder to predict and less suitable for insurance. For example, the risk of losing a job varies with the economy, making it challenging to forecast. Conversely, the number of houses that catch fire within a year in a specific area is more stable and predictable.

2.7. Understanding Fire Insurance: Its Purpose, Benefits, and Coverage

Fire insurance is a type of coverage where an individual pays a premium to an insurance company in exchange for financial protection against losses caused by fire.

This insurance offers protection for residential and commercial properties, including homes, apartments, furniture, and business buildings. Fire insurance reimburses the policyholder for the cost of replacing or repairing damaged property and belongings that were destroyed by fire.

2.7.1. Key Concepts of Fire Insurance

- **Indemnity:** This refers to the coverage that only compensates for the loss.
- **Proximate Cause:** This is the direct cause of the fire.
- **Insurable Interest:** This means the policyholder must own the property or belongings being insured.

2.7.2. Benefits of Fire Insurance for Homeowners

- Coverage for Building Damage
- Compensation for Home Furnishings: This includes items like furniture, carpets, and clothing that are damaged by fire.
- Coverage for Electronic Equipment: This includes appliances and devices like televisions and computers that are damaged by fire.

2.7.3. Benefits of Fire Insurance for Businesses

- Coverage for Commercial Property Damage
- Compensation for Share Damage
- Coverage for Employee Death Benefits
- Coverage for Machinery and Equipment Damage
- Coverage for Employee Medical Expenses

Fire incidents are unpredictable but can cause significant damage. Therefore, having fire insurance is crucial for protection.

2.7.4. What is Covered by Fire Insurance?

- Factories: This includes electrical systems, machinery, and inventory.
- Homes: This covers personal belongings, excluding high-value or precious items.
- Shops and Hotels: This includes furniture and inventory.

However, fire insurance does not cover:

- Earthquakes
- Wars
- Terrorism
- Damage caused by others (for example, if a fire is started by someone else's property)

2.7.5. Calculating Fire Insurance Claims

To determine the insurance claim for the financial loss resulting from a fire-related business interruption, the following procedures must be implemented:

Short Sale: A short sale refers to the reduction in sales caused by a fire incident and the resulting business interruption. This is defined as the gap between the expected standard sales and the actual sales during the indemnity period. This concept is demonstrated through the following example.

Date of Fire occurs	01-06-2013
Period of dislocation of business	4 months
Standard Sale	500,00
Increased trend	15%
Actual Sale	3,00,000

Example: Compute the short sale based on the details provided above:

Standard turnover (Rs. 50,000+15%) (A)	5,75,000
Less: Actual Sale(B)	3,00,000
Short Sale(A-B)	2,75,000

Solution

Reduction in Costs: Any savings made as a result of a fire will be subtracted from the total amount determined previously.

Standard Clause: Should the insured amount be lower than the policy's value, the standard clause will be utilized, as previously mentioned for the stock insurance.

2.7.6. Accounting Entries

In case of loss of stock

<table>
<tr><td>

Insurance Company A/c Dr.

    To Stock Damage A/c

    To Stock Destroyed A/c

(Being claim admitted for stock destroyed and stock damaged)

</td></tr>
<tr><td>

Stock Destroyed A/c Dr.

Stock Damaged A/c Dr.

    To Trading A/c

(Being actual cost of stock destroyed and stock damaged to trading account)

</td></tr>
<tr><td>

Bank A/c Dr.

    To Stock Damaged A/c

(Being realisation made on sale of damaged stock)

</td></tr>
</table>

Entries to be noted

Note: Difference of stock destroyed account and damaged account will be transferred to profit & loss a/c

In case of loss of profit

<table>
<tr><td>

Insurance company A/c Dr.

    To Profit & Loss A/c

    To Profit & Loss Suspense A/c

(Being loss of profit for next year)

</td></tr>
<tr><td>

Bank A/c Dr.

    To Insurance Company A/c

(Being amount received from Insurance Company)

</td></tr>
</table>

Entries to be noted

2.8. Marine Insurance Policy and Certificate

Marine insurance protects against the loss or damage of ships, their cargo, terminals, and any means of transportation involved in the transfer, acquisition, or storage of the property from its starting point to its destination. Cargo insurance is a specific section of marine insurance that also covers property exposed to both onshore and offshore risks, including container terminals, ports, oil platforms, pipelines, hull damage, marine casualty, and marine liability. When items are transported via mail or courier, shipping insurance is utilized instead.

General Average

In the context of marine insurance, "general average" refers to the fair distribution of expenses or losses among all parties involved in a maritime operation. For general average to be declared correctly, the following conditions must be met:

    a. There must be an event that is beyond the control of the shipowner but endangers the entire voyage.
    b. There must be a deliberate act of sacrifice.
    c. There must be something of value saved.

The act of sacrifice could involve the deliberate disposal of certain cargo, the use of tugs, salvage operations, or damage to the ship, whether it be through voluntary grounding or knowingly operating the engines that could cause damage. General average requires all participants in the maritime venture (including the ship's hull, cargo, freight, and bunkers) to contribute to rectifying the sacrifice. They share in the cost based on the 'value at risk' of the voyage. Partial loss, whether it affects the ship's hull or its cargo, is referred to as 'particular average.'

Under-Insurance

This term is used when the insured has not adequately insured an item, meaning they have insured it for less than its actual value. In such cases, under-insurance will be considered, and the claim amount will be reduced accordingly.

An adjuster specializing in general average is responsible for handling the adjustment and issuing the general average statement. In North America, such adjusters are members of the 'association of Average Adjusters' to ensure the process is fair. The appointment of a General Average adjuster is made by the shipowner, who is then compensated by the insurer.

2.9. Specialized Policies

A variety of specialized policies are available, including:

- **Construction site damage protection:** This policy protects against damage to the ship's structure while it's being built.
- **Cargo insurance for the shipper:** This policy can be purchased by a carrier, freight broker, or the goods' owner as protection for the goods. If the goods are lost or damaged, this insurance will cover their true value, not just the legal liability of the carrier.
- **Yacht insurance:** This type of insurance, also known as pleasure craft insurance, includes coverage for liability. Smaller boats like yachts and fishing vessels are typically insured under a "binding authority" or "line slip" agreement.
- **Coverage for war risks:** Standard hull insurance does not cover the risks of a ship entering a war zone. For instance, a tanker in the Persian Gulf during the Gulf War was at risk of war damage. The areas at risk for war damage are set by the London-based Joint War Committee, which has recently expanded to include the Malacca Straits due to piracy concerns. If an incident is considered a "riot," it would be covered by war risk insurers.
- **Increased Value (IV) coverage:** This coverage safeguards the shipowner from any difference between the insured value of the vessel and its market value.
- **Overdue insurance:** This form of insurance is now largely outdated due to improvements in communication technology. It was an early form of reinsurance and was taken out by an insurer when a ship arrived late at its destination port, risking loss but also the possibility of delay. The Titanic's overdue insurance was famously handled by Lloyd's.
- **Insurance for cargo:** Cargo insurance is based on the Institute Cargo Clauses, with coverage rated A, B, or C, with A offering the broadest coverage and C the narrowest. Specialized insurance exists for certain types of cargo, like valuable goods, known as specie. There are also specific insurance conditions for certain cargo types, such as frozen food, frozen meat, bulk commodities like oil, coal, and jute. These conditions are often developed for specific groups, like the Institute Federation of Oils, Seeds, and Fats Associations (FOFSA) Trades Clauses, which have been established with the FOFSA. Additionally, there are discussions on developing insurance policies to address plastic pollution from cargo losses at sea. For example, marine insurance policies should include coverage for liability for marine plastic pollution, marine clean-up, and conservation.

2.10. Underlying Causes and Out-of-Pocket Expenses

Marine insurance policies are typically written on an occurrence basis, which means they cover damages or injuries that occur during the policy period, regardless of when the claim is filed. These policies often include additional coverage for common risks faced by marine businesses, such as liability for damages to containers and the removal of debris.

A deductible is the initial amount that the policyholder is responsible for paying out of pocket before the insurance company steps in. While it's possible to have no deductible, it's more common for marine insurance policies to have deductibles for claims filed under them.

2.11. Certificate of Marine Insurance

A certificate of marine insurance is a document provided by the insured to the shipping company or any other entity responsible for their cargo or shipping activities. It serves as proof that the cargo is insured while it's being transported and is backed by a copy of the insurance policy. This document is also referred to as a special cargo policy or a cargo insurance certificate.

This certificate is issued under an open policy (also known as open cover) insurance. An open policy outlines a specific timeframe during which the insured's marine business is protected by the insurer when shipping their cargo to a particular shipper or carrier. Essentially, it informs the shipper that the shipping operation is insured.

Although the certificate is issued by the insured, it is supported by a copy of the insurance policy from the insurer, which will soon be provided.

Certificate of Insurance: This document proves the existence of insurance coverage but does not detail the specific terms and conditions of the insurance policy. It is also known as a 'Cover Note'.

Insurance Broker's Note: This document indicates that insurance has been arranged, but it does not constitute a formal insurance contract.

2.11.1. Coverage of Fire and Marine Insurance Policies

Details of Coverage for Basic Fire and Special Perils Insurance Policies

I. Fire Coverage

This includes protection against fire damage or destruction not caused by:

- Natural heating, or spontaneous combustion, own fermentation of insured property
- The property undergoing any heating or drying processes
- Damage or destruction from fires set by any government authority

II. Lightning Coverage

Protection against damage or destruction from lightning strikes, excluding:

- Damage or destruction to boilers (excluding those used in homes), economizers, or any vessels where steam is produced, machinery or equipment affected by their own explosion or implosion,
- Damage or destruction from aircraft, other airborne or space devices, or items dropped from them due to pressure waves.

III. Aircraft Damage Coverage

Protection against damage or destruction from aircraft, other airborne or space devices, and items dropped from them, except for damage caused by pressure waves.

IV. Damage from Aircraft

Protection against damage or destruction from aircraft, other airborne or space devices, and items dropped from them, except for damage caused by pressure waves.

V. Damage from Riot, Strike, and Malicious Intent

Protection against visible physical damage or destruction from violent acts directly affecting the insured property, excluding:

- Damage or destruction from the complete or partial stoppage of work, the slowing down, interruption, or cessation of any process or operations, or any omissions by the insured or their employees
- Damage or destruction from the permanent or temporary loss of property due to confiscation, commandeering, requisition, or destruction by government or any legally recognized authority
- Damage or destruction from the permanent or temporary loss of property due to the unlawful occupation of buildings, plants, units, or machinery, or the blocking of access to them
- Damage or destruction from burglary, housebreaking, theft, larceny, or any similar act or omission by any person.

VI. Damage from Impact

Damage or destruction from any vehicle or animal, not owned by the insured or any person on the insured's premises, or their employees while performing their duties.

2.11.2. Understanding Marine Insurance

The essence and breadth of marine insurance are defined by the Marine Insurance Act and the terms "marine adventure" and "maritime perils".

- It involves a promise of compensation, but the level of compensation is set by the agreement.
- It covers damages related to a maritime adventure or to the construction, maintenance, or launch of a vessel.
- A maritime adventure occurs when the insured property faces risks from the sea.
- Maritime perils are risks that come from or are related to sea navigation.

2.11.3. Liability, Personal Accident, and Specialty Insurance

Liability Insurance

Liability insurance is an insurance coverage that shields the insured from financial liabilities arising from injuries or damage to others' property. This type of insurance covers legal expenses and any compensation the insured party might have to pay if they are legally responsible. It does not cover damages caused on purpose or contractual liabilities. Unlike other insurance types, liability insurance pays out to third parties, not the policyholder.

Liability insurance, also known as third-party insurance, is a component of the broader insurance system aimed at managing risks by protecting the insured from liability claims from lawsuits and similar legal actions. It also safeguards the insured if they are sued for claims that fall within the policy's coverage.

Originally, companies facing a shared risk would pool their resources to create a self-help fund for compensation in the event of a loss (this was known as a mutual insurance arrangement). Today, the system is more structured, with specialized insurance companies offering protection against specific risks in exchange for a premium.

Liability insurance is specifically designed to protect against claims from third parties, meaning the insurance company pays out to the claimant, not the insured. Generally, it does not cover damages caused intentionally or contractual liabilities. When a claim is filed, the insurance company is obligated to defend the insured.

The insurance company is not responsible for the legal costs of the defence unless the policy explicitly states otherwise. This rule is beneficial because defence costs often increase significantly during legal proceedings. In many instances, the defence portion of the policy can be more valuable than the insurance itself, especially in complex cases where the cost of defending the case might exceed the claim amount, particularly in "nuisance" cases where the insured must defend even if no liability is proven in court.

Categories

In numerous nations, having liability insurance is a mandatory requirement for individuals who could face legal action from others for being negligent. The primary categories of such policies typically include drivers of vehicles (also known as vehicle insurance), professionals offering services to the public, manufacturers of potentially dangerous products, builders, and employers. The rationale behind these regulations is that these groups are involved in activities that could potentially harm others, necessitating insurance coverage to ensure compensation can be provided if their actions lead to losses or damages to others. Moreover, there are additional types of risks that people seek protection against, leading to an expansion in the variety and number of liability policies as the prevalence of contingency fee legal services has increased, sometimes on a collective action basis.

Public Liability

The operations and activities of industries and businesses can impact various parties, including the general public (consumers, visitors, trespassers, subcontractors, etc.), who might suffer physical injuries or have their property damaged or both. The legal status of making employer's liability insurance and public liability insurance compulsory varies by state. Regardless of legal mandates, many organizations elect to include public liability insurance in their insurance coverage, despite the complexities of the standard policies, such as conditions, exclusions, and guarantees. For example, a company operating an industrial site might purchase insurance for product pollution to protect against legal claims arising from environmental incidents.

Product Liability Insurance

While not all countries require product liability insurance, laws like the UK Consumer Protection Act 1987 and the EC Directive on Product Liability mandate that manufacturers or suppliers of goods have some form of product liability insurance, often as part of a broader liability policy. The potential for significant liability is demonstrated by instances like those involving Mercedes-Benz with unstable vehicles and Perrier with benzene contamination, but the list of covered products is extensive, ranging from pharmaceuticals and medical devices to asbestos, tobacco, recreational items, machinery and electronics, chemicals and pesticides, agricultural tools and equipment, food contaminated with harmful substances, and all major product categories.

Personal Accident Insurance

Personal accident insurance offers coverage for medical expenses and compensation in the event of disability or death due to accidents. If the policyholder passes away in an accident, their nominee receives compensation for accidental death. This ensures the family's financial stability in such unfortunate circumstances. The compensation amount can range from Rs 5 lakh to Rs 1 crore.

Permanent Total Disability from an Accident: In some instances, even with medical assistance, a person may become permanently disabled. In such cases, the insurance policy will provide a certain sum of money based on the type of disability. This policy also includes coverage for permanent loss of speech, vision in both eyes, and hearing in both ears.

Permanent Partial Disability

This applies when an individual has experienced a partial loss of hearing in one ear, vision in one eye, or has lost an index finger, thumb, or an entire hand. In these situations, the insured individual can file a claim with the insurance company.

Transportation Benefit: Certain insurance companies also offer a benefit for transportation to the family. For example, if the insured person is hospitalized more than 150 km from their home, the insurance will cover the transportation costs up to a maximum of Rs 50,000 for the immediate family members.

Additional Benefits

The insurance policy also includes coverage for other aspects such as educational and employment benefits, as well as funeral expenses. It also covers hospital bills, including the cost of ambulance services. Some policies provide allowances for education and benefits for home or vehicle modifications.

Specialty Insurance

This type of insurance is designed for unique or special circumstances that are not typically covered by standard insurance policies. It includes coverage for items like powersports vehicles, educational liability, and specialized homeowners' insurance for properties with aging roofs.

Specialty insurance policies are tailored for businesses that require special coverage. These policies are often needed by businesses with high-risk assets or that deal with items not usually covered by basic policies. For instance, insurance for guns and antiques is essential for proper protection of investments.

Any business catering to clients involved in high-risk activities must explore specialty insurance options. For example, a skydiving company is considered high risk and may face more liability claims. Construction companies are another example of businesses that typically opt for specialty insurance to mitigate the risk of lawsuits.

- Specialty insurance is designed for businesses with unique needs. Industries such as construction, environmental, healthcare, and energy are examples of specialty insurance sectors.
- The cost of specialty insurance quotes varies based on the industry and the level of risk your business faces in terms of lawsuits. Adding an umbrella policy can increase the maximum payout of your plan.

Health Insurance

India faces numerous health challenges. It has been labelled as the diabetes capital of the globe. Every year, approximately one million new cancer patients are diagnosed, and the increasing prevalence of non-communicable diseases (NCDs) accounts for 61% of all deaths in the nation. Undoubtedly, advancements in medicine are bringing new hope to the healthcare industry. However, these advancements are also leading to a surge in healthcare costs. The expenses associated with diagnosis, medication, treatment, and hospital stays are causing significant financial strain, making it unaffordable for the average person. Consequently, individuals are often forced to sell their assets or borrow money in the event of a medical emergency, leading to financial hardship for their families. To address these health crises, we provide Mediclaim insurance that not only protects you from potential risks but also offers financial assistance when you need it most.

Advantages

a. It offers the convenience of cashless hospitalization during a medical emergency.

b. It allows for tax deductions under Section 80D of the Income Tax Act, up to Rs.1,00,000 for the premium paid on a family floater policy, based on the proposer and insured's age.

c. It includes additional features such as the option for an international second opinion, tailored to meet your healthcare needs for comprehensive protection.

d. It covers medical expenses before and after hospitalization, including outpatient visits, diagnosis, doctor's fees, medication, therapies, and more. It will cover a wide range of out-of-pocket medical expenses.

e. It provides the option for lifelong renewability, along with additional benefits like coverage for alternative treatments, day care procedures, annual health check-ups, etc.

f. You have the freedom to choose a hospital that accepts your insurance on a cashless basis at nearby in-network facilities.

g. It offers coverage for medical expenses before and after hospitalization.

h. Claims can be settled through a cashless facility or by reimbursement up to the sum insured.

a. It includes coverage for in-patient hospital stays.

j. It provides lifelong renewability with extra benefits, such as coverage for alternative treatments, day care procedures, annual health check-ups, etc.

k. You can access advanced medical treatments on a cashless basis at any in-network hospitals nearby.

Features:

a. It covers medical expenses before and after hospitalization.

b. Claims can be settled through a cashless facility or by reimbursement up to the sum insured.

c. It includes coverage for in-patient hospital stays.

d. You can choose a hospital that accepts your insurance on a cashless basis at nearby in-network facilities.

Various Mediclaim Policies

a. **Individual Mediclaim:** This plan is designed for a single person, offering coverage for a specific amount of money. The insured individual can use the policy's benefits and the full sum insured amount for their medical expenses, as long as the premium is paid.

b. **Family Floater Mediclaim Cover:** This policy is for a family, allowing all members, including spouses, children, and parents, to benefit from the coverage and benefits. It has a shared sum insured, which can be used by any family member for hospitalization or medical treatments.

c. **Critical Illness Mediclaim:** This policy is for those facing long-term medical treatments that could result in very high medical bills. It covers serious illnesses like stroke, cancer, and heart disease, among others, with coverage for up to 32 critical illnesses.

d. **Senior Citizen Mediclaim Policy:** This policy is tailored for individuals aged 60 and above, offering coverage and benefits for hospitalization and medical services.

e. **Heart Mediclaim:** This plan provides comprehensive coverage for hospitalization and medical treatments related to heart conditions, helping to alleviate financial burdens. It covers 16 major heart conditions.

f. **Cancer Mediclaim:** This policy offers lifelong protection and extensive coverage for cancer treatments, including chemotherapy and radiotherapy, making it a wise investment for those at risk.

Mediclaim Benefits:

a. **Day Care Treatments:** If you need surgery, treatment, or therapy that requires a day in the hospital, we cover all daycare treatment expenses up to the sum insured. We offer the highest coverage for daycare treatments in the market.

b. **In-Patient Hospitalization:** If you stay in the hospital for more than 24 hours, we cover all the expenses, including room charges, nursing fees, ICIJ, surgeon's fees, doctor's fees, blood, oxygen, and operating theatre changes.

c. **ICU Charges:** We believe in the value of every life and the importance of quality healthcare. If you're in ICU, we'll cover the ICU charges.

d. **Ambulance Cover:** This policy reimburses you for ambulance expenses during a medical emergency.

e. **Pre and Post Hospitalization:** This includes coverage for the costs of diagnosis, treatment, and medication before and after hospitalization, along with doctor's fees.

f. **Recharge of Sum Insured:** If your coverage amount is used up, you'll get it automatically replenished, which can be used for the treatment of other family members or yourself.

g. **Other Benefits:** This includes coverage for organ donation, second opinion, NCB, and alternative treatments.

h. **Annual Health Check-Ups:** As part of the Mediclaim plan, you'll have access to an annual health check-up at our approved healthcare providers. This includes tests like complete blood count, urine analysis, kidney function tests, and ECG checks.

2.12. Health Insurance Rules, 2016; Health and Life Integration Products

The Insurance Regulatory and Development Authority of India (IRDAI) has made several updates to health insurance regulations. On July 18, 2016, the Authority updated the Health Insurance Regulations, 2013, and issued the Health Insurance Regulations, 2016. These updates include the establishment of a Product Management Committee (PMC) for both General and Health Insurers, which serves as a company's internal review body. The PMC is responsible for approving the launch of Group Insurance products through the Use and File process and for the withdrawal of products. Approval from IRDAI is no longer required for Group Health Insurance Products and the withdrawal of products by General and Health Insurers. The new rules enhance transparency and flexibility in the withdrawal and introduction of products.

2.12.1. Main Alterations in IRDAI (Health Insurance) Regulations, 2016

- The Health Plus Life Combi Product allows for the combination of any Life Insurance coverage provided by a life insurer with Health Insurance coverage from a General or Health Insurer.
- General or Health Insurers are allowed to introduce pilot products for a duration not exceeding five years. After five years from the product's launch, it must either continue as a standard product or be discontinued.
- Life Insurers are permitted to offer long-term Individual Health Insurance policies, with terms of 5 years or more. However, indemnity-based products are not allowed.
- Credit Linked Group Health/Personal Accident policies can be offered for a duration up to the loan term, which does not exceed five years, by all insurers.
- Health Insurance Products must be marketed or offered only after they have been filed with the Authority in accordance with the Product Filing Guidelines. These guidelines outline the Use and File requirements for Group Health Insurance Products from both General and Health Insurers.

- The Product Management Committee (PMC) of General and Health Insurers has the authority to approve the withdrawal of a Health Product by adhering to the existing Guidelines outlined in the Product Filing Guidelines, 2016.
- After five years, there is no requirement to seek new approval for product performance reviews.

Guidelines for Group Insurance are specified.

- General and Health Insurers are encouraged to implement mechanisms or incentives to reward policyholders for adopting wellness and preventive health habits. It is also specified that the underwriting policy should cover the approach and aspects related to offering health insurance coverage to both standard and sub-standard lives, with denial of a proposal being the final step.
- Insurers are now allowed to use the same application form for any number of their products, with norms in place to protect the privacy of policyholders.
- The restriction on allowing Cumulative Bonus for Benefit-Based Products has been removed.
- General and Health Insurers are tasked with making efforts to provide coverage for one or more systems under the AYUSH. The exemption for Benefit-Based Products has also been removed.
- Norms on the Wellness and Preventive Aspects of Health Insurance Products have been specified.
- The terminology for 'Standard List of Excluded Expenses in Hospitalization Indemnity Policies' has been updated to 'Items for which optional cover may be offered by Insurers' to allow Insurers to cover these typically excluded items at their discretion.
- Policyholders have the right to request the settlement of their claim in accordance with the terms of their policies.
- There is no requirement for new underwriting at the renewal stage when there are no changes in the Sum Insured offered. Should there be an improvement in the risk profile, the Insurer may consider recognizing this for the removal of any loadings at the renewal stage.
- The previous regulatory provision for HIR, 2013 [Reg. No. on claim events occurring during two policy periods has been removed. No claim should be closed by the Insurer's records without proper disposal in accordance with the terms and conditions of the policy.

Additional information that must be shared includes:

- Details about the products or services offered by TPAs, either by type, location, or region.
- Details regarding the cashless services provided by the products.
- A list of Network Providers by geographical area.
- Specific information related to Pilot Products.
- In the event of a Pilot Product, the necessary disclosures must be made.
- The Insurer is responsible for providing a permanent identity card (such as Smart Cards) for the use of cashless services, which remains valid as long as the policy is continued with the company.
- The Insurer sets certain standards and criteria for hospitals within the provider network through guidelines.
- In the event that a claim is rejected or denied, the insurer is the only entity allowed to communicate the reason for the rejection, which should be based on the policy conditions. The company should also provide information on the grievance redressal procedures available, including those with the Insurance Ombudsman.
- Insurers and TPAs are required to establish systems and procedures to identify, monitor, and prevent fraud.

2.13. Health and Life Integration Products

All Life Insurance and Non-Life Insurance Companies are authorized to promote 'Integration Products'. These 'Integration Products' are the amalgamation of Term Life Insurance policies provided by life insurance companies and Health Insurance policies offered by non-life insurance companies. For the purpose of this category, Health Insurance refers to policies that exclusively provide coverage for sickness benefits or benefits related to medical, surgical, or hospital expenses, whether they are received in a hospital setting or not, on a payment for service or reimbursement basis.

- The limits for Policy Term and Sum Assured are set as per the proposal and approved under File and Use regulations.
- Additional coverage options, known as 'Riders / Add-on Covers', can be included, subject to approval under File and Use regulations.
- The cost of both risks must be clearly distinguished and explained to policyholders at both the time of purchase and at any later stage, in all relevant documents such as the policy agreement and sales materials.
- These products can be sold individually or as part of a group policy. However, for health insurance floater policies, the term life insurance coverage is permitted for the life of a family's earning member who is also the policyholder of the health insurance policy, provided there is an insurable interest and the policy complies with the underwriting standards of the insurer.
- The total premium amount for the 'Integration Product' will determine the threshold limits or applicability of existing Regulations, guidelines, and circulars issued by the regulatory authority or any other statutory entity.
- Claims and commission payments for 'Integration Products' are the responsibility of the respective insurance companies.
- The 'Integration Product' is subject to a free look period, as specified in Regulation (6) (2) of the IRDA (Protection of Policyholders' Interests) Regulations, 2002. This free look period applies to the entire 'Integration Product'.
- The health component of the 'Integration Product' allows the policyholder to choose to have an independent or stand-alone health insurance policy from a non-life insurance company, at the policyholder's discretion.

2.14. Primary Insurer

Given that two insurance firms are involved in the provision of the 'Combi Product', one of these firms may be mutually agreed upon to serve as the primary insurer for each 'Combi Product' sold, provided that the terms, conditions, and considerations are mutually agreed upon. The primary insurer, for the purpose of these guidelines, is the insurance firm that both insurers have mutually agreed upon to play a pivotal role in facilitating the policy service as a point of contact for providing various services as outlined in these guidelines. It is anticipated that the primary insurer will play a significant role in overseeing the underwriting and policy service aspects.

- **Underwriting:** For the 'Combi Product', the risk associated with each component will be managed by the respective insurance companies involved. Specifically, the risk related to life insurance will be managed by the Life Insurance Company, while the risk related to the health insurance portion will be managed by the Non-Life Insurance Company.
- **Filing and Utilization:** It is expected that the combined strengths of both insurers will be utilized, with the resulting benefits being shared with the policyholders of this product category. Therefore, it is proposed that the individual insurance products be merged into a single product, which will be filed under a unified brand name. Both insurers are encouraged to conduct a cost-benefit analysis from the perspective of the common policyholders before submitting the product for approval. The insurance companies may also use existing insurance products (that are not modified and are already approved under the current File and Use standards). However, the 'Combi Product' will be submitted for File and Use approval at the time of integration, regardless of any prior approval for either of the individual products. The filing of the 'Combi Product' will adhere to the current File and Use guidelines, as well as any future guidelines that may be issued. The 'Combi Product' will be

submitted to the Actuarial Department of IRDA in File and Use formats that are currently in use.

2.14.1. Diverse Types of Unusual Insurance Policies

- **Mobile Insurance:** The advent of mobile phones has occurred rapidly, transforming them from simple devices to high-value gadgets that can range from a few thousand to tens of thousands of dollars. Mobile insurance protects you from the financial burden of expensive repairs, replacements, and theft. Our phones have become deeply personal, making it crucial to secure them with the best mobile insurance options available.
- **Marine Insurance:** The ocean presents numerous hazards, including severe weather, water damage, and piracy. Insurance providers offer coverage for ships and boats through cargo insurance, freight insurance, and hull insurance. Marine insurance not only shields the vessel but also the goods being transported, providing financial security. Discover the top marine insurance policies tailored to your specific needs.
- **Crop Insurance:** Agriculture is the foundation of human society, providing essential food. However, it is a risky industry due to natural disasters, inflation, and damage to farming equipment. Crop insurance helps protect farmers from any losses or damages to their crops and property. Find the ideal crop insurance policy for your agricultural needs.
- **Property Insurance:** Property insurance is a broad category of general insurance that benefits those who own property, assets, equipment, and cargo. It covers all risks associated with both movable and immovable assets, theft, and damage.
- **Liability Insurance:** Liability insurance addresses specific requirements in situations where individuals or businesses need protection against legal claims related to negligence, malpractice, or injury. Certain business activities carry significant risks, making it essential for employers to consider insuring themselves or their business against these risks.
- **Commercial Vehicle Insurance:** Commercial vehicles are crucial assets for businesses, and the cost of accidents, damages, theft, and other risks can be substantial. Commercial Vehicle Insurance is specifically designed to protect you against these risks, ensuring your business doesn't suffer financial losses due to unforeseen events.
- **Annuities Insurance:** A comfortable retirement is a common goal, and insurance companies provide schemes to ensure financial stability after retirement. Annuity is an investment product that guarantees a steady income for a certain period or until your passing.
- **Laptop Insurance:** Laptops have become invaluable due to their high cost and the sensitive information they store. Damage or theft of a laptop can lead to significant financial losses. Although laptop insurance is not widely chosen, it can be beneficial in the event of loss. Explore the various laptop insurance options available to find the best policy for you.
- **Business Insurance:** Cover a wide range of business-related risks. Safeguard your business financially against unexpected events affecting your property, employees, assets, and any potential legal issues. Explore the best coverage options from leading providers before choosing the right policy for your business.
- **Business Credit Insurance:** Protect your business when engaging in credit transactions with others or extending credit to customers. This insurance offers stability and reassurance when making purchases on credit and simplifies the process of extending credit to customers.
- **Homeowner's Insurance:** Our home is a valuable asset vulnerable to various threats. Ensure your home is protected against natural disasters, theft, fire, and other emergencies to facilitate the recovery process. These policies also cover your personal belongings, safeguarding your lifestyle.
- **Pet Insurance:** Consider insuring your pet to cover veterinary bills for any health issues or injuries. Additionally, these policies provide financial support if your pet is lost or passes away, covering the cost of the funeral.
- **Product Liability Insurance:** Should your business face claims related to personal injury or property damage from your products, this insurance can shield you from legal action and associated legal fees. It covers the expenses

related to compensation claims.

- **Mortgage Insurance:** Mortgage insurance is crucial for two main reasons: it protects your mortgage in the event of non-payment and can make you eligible for a loan if you don't meet the usual criteria. Obtaining this insurance ensures your credit score remains intact if you fall behind on payments.
- **Disability Insurance:** Should you suffer an injury, whether temporary or permanent, that affects your ability to work, disability insurance can replace a portion of your income, providing a stable financial base. This insurance is particularly vital for those in high-risk occupations.
- **Rural Insurance:** The insurance needs of those living in rural areas differ from urban areas. These policies are tailored to meet the specific needs of rural communities, covering personal health, critical illnesses, weather-related losses, livestock protection, and more.
- **Professional Liability Insurance:** Designed for companies offering complex advice or services that could lead to legal issues, Professional Liability Insurance covers legal defence costs. It is also known as Errors and Omissions Insurance.
- **Child Insurance:** The cost of raising a child is so high that having insurance is essential for ensuring their future financial security. These policies are designed to meet the specific needs of each child, making them highly flexible and tailored. Explore the benefits of these insurance policies and choose the one that best suits your child's needs.
- **Building Insurance:** Homeowners' insurance protects the structure of your home and its permanent features. This coverage includes the home's framework, such as walls, floors, roofs, and windows, as well as the fixtures in the bathroom, bedroom, and kitchen. However, this insurance does not cover the items inside the home and is more appropriate for those who wish to insure only the building itself.

IMPORTANT QUESTIONS

Short Answer Questions (5 marks each):

1. List and briefly explain the fundamental principles of insurance.
2. What is the concept of insurable interest and why is it important?
3. Explain the principle of indemnity in insurance contracts.
4. Describe the concept of subrogation and its implications for insurers.
5. What is the principle of utmost good faith and how does it impact insurance contracts?

Long Answer Questions (15 marks each):

1. Discuss the different types of life insurance products available and their key features.
2. Explain the concept of linked insurance policies and their advantages and disadvantages.
3. Describe the features of annuities and group insurance policies.
4. List the different types of risks faced by asset owners and how general insurance products provide coverage.
5. Explain the concept of perils and discuss the features of insurance products covering fire and allied perils.
6. Describe the features of insurance products that cover marine and transit risks.
7. Discuss various insurance products that offer financial protection in case of accidents.
8. Analyze how health insurance products provide financial assistance during hospitalization.
9. Explain different insurance products that cover miscellaneous risks.

10. Choose a specific insurance product (e.g., health insurance) and explain its features, benefits, and exclusions.

OBJECTIVE TYPE QUESTIONS

Multiple Choice Questions (MCQs)

1. Which principle states that the insured must have a financial stake in the insured property?

   a) Principle of Indemnity
   b) Principle of Insurable Interest
   c) Principle of Subrogation
   d) Principle of Contribution
   2. An annuity plan provides income:
   a) Only upon death of the policyholder
   b) Only during the term of the policy
   c) Regularly after a certain period
   d) None of the above

3. Marine insurance covers risks associated with:

   a) Buildings
   b) Vehicles
   c) Goods transported by sea
   d) Personal accidents

4. Which of the following is NOT a general insurance product?

   a) Term life insurance
   b) Fire insurance
   c) Health insurance
   d) Motor insurance

5. Group insurance policies are typically offered by:

   a) Individuals
   b) Employers or associations
   c) Government agencies
   d) All of the above

6. Perils refer to:

   a) unexpected events causing financial loss
   b) Types of insurance policies
   c) Investment options
   d) Benefits offered by an insurance policy

7. Endowment plans provide:

   a) Life insurance coverage only
   b) Maturity benefits along with life insurance coverage
   c) Investment benefits with no life insurance coverage
   d) Both a and c

8. The principle of utmost good faith requires both the insurer and the insured to disclose all information.

   a) relevant
   b) personal
   c) financial
   d) medical

9. Term plans provide coverage for a period in exchange for premiums.

   a) specified
   b) lifetime
   c) maturity
   d) hospitalization

10. A combination plan offers both protection and savings benefits.

    a) Term
    b) Pure Endowment
    c) Unit Linked
    d) Annuity

11. Traditional life insurance products focus on guaranteed benefits, while linked policies offer market-linked returns.

    a) Unit
    b) Term
    c) Endowment
    d) Annuity

12. Fire insurance protects against damage caused by fire and related perils.

    a) Marine
    b) Health
    c) Liability
    d) Travel

13. Personal accident insurance provides financial assistance in case of accidental injuries.

    a) Vehicle
    b) Property
    c) Travel

d) Medical

14. Hospitalization insurance covers expenses incurred during a hospital stay.

    a) Critical Illness
    b) Accident
    c) Travel
    d) Property

15. Products covering miscellaneous risks could include theft insurance or cyber insurance.

    a) True
    b) False

Fill up the Blanks

1. The principle of _____________ ensures the insured is not financially better off after a claim.
2. Disclosure of _____________ information is crucial for a fair insurance contract.
3. _____________ plans provide life insurance coverage for a specific period.
4. Traditional insurance products focus on _____________ benefits, while linked policies offer _____________ benefits as well.
5. _____________ insurance covers risks associated with property damage caused by fire and related events.
6. In the event of a claim, the principle of limits the insurer's payout to the actual financial loss suffered. (Indemnity)
7. The principle of allows the insurer to step into the shoes of the insured to recover compensation from a third party. (Subrogation)
8. Pure endowment plans focus on building a at maturity. (corpus)
9. Unit-linked policies offer the potential for returns alongside life cover. (market-linked)
10. Annuities are a good option for individuals seeking a regular income in their years. (retirement)
11. _____________ insurance plans reimburse hospitalization expenses. (Medical)
12. _____________ insurance covers risks associated with travel, such as trip cancellation or medical emergencies. (Travel)
13. _____________ policies can protect against theft of personal belongings. (Property)
14. _____________ insurance safeguards businesses against data breaches and cyberattacks. (Cyber)
15. General insurance products are designed to protect against _____________ losses. (Financial)

ANSWERS

Multiple Choice Questions

1. (b) Principle of Insurable Interest
2. (d) Principle of Contribution
3. (a) relevant
4. (a) specified

5. (c) Unit Linked
6. (a) Unit
7. (a) guaranteed
8. (d) Travel
9. (c) Goods transported by sea
10. (a) Term life insurance
11. (b) Employers or associations
12. (a) unexpected events causing financial loss
13. (b) Maturity benefits along with life insurance coverage
14. (a) relevant
15. (b) False

Fill in the Blanks

1. Indemnity
2. Relevant
3. Term
4. Guaranteed, market-linked
5. Fire and allied perils
6. Indemnity
7. Subrogation
8. Corpus
9. Market-Linked
10. Retirement
11. Medical
12. Travel
13. Property
14. Cyber
15. Financial

xXxXxXx